SIGNS OF FAITH

BIBLE VERSES FOR
PRETEENS AND YOUTH

By **Marcia Stoner**

Illustrated by **John Jordan**

Copy-edited by **Martha Hutchinson**

Designed by **Gillian Housewright**

Signing Consultant **Charles Robert Geldreich**

Abingdon Press
Nashville

SIGNS of FAITH

BIBLE VERSES FOR PRETEENS AND YOUTH

SIGNS FOR

BIBLE VERSE

LEARNING AND PRESENTATION

This book is dedicated to Bob Geldreich, a man who gives of himself to open the world to others. Without Bob's invaluable help this book could never have come to life. Bob has taught sign language at Brentwood United Methodist Church in Brentwood, Tennessee, and is an active participant in the League for the Deaf and Hard of Hearing.

Preteens and youth are usually not too eager to memorize Bible verses. However, learning to sign a Bible verse for a worship service or other setting can be both challenging and fun—and remembering the Bible verse is an added benefit.

SIGNS OF FAITH

will help preteens and youth learn to sign Bible verses using the hand motions of American Sign Language. *Signs of Faith* can help you in your efforts to make worship a memorable experience for your students, especially when you find a setting appropriate for them to sign the verses for others. Signing Bible verses not only makes a great worship enhancement for the whole congregation, but also gives your students the opportunity to provide a service to your church.

While you might be intimidated at the thought of signing the many words to countless Bible verses, remember that words as well as signs are repeated often. *Signs of Faith* provides clear illustrations of the sign for each word as well as written instructions for signing (but be aware that the written instructions for each word appear only with the first instance of the word within each verse). Also note that in religious signing the *meaning* of the passage is signed, not necessarily the exact words. For example, different denominations might have different signs for the word *baptize.*

Use the simple steps listed below to learn these verses yourself and then teach the verses to your preteens and youth:

- Look at the illustrations. (Follow the illustrations on each page from top to bottom, starting at the top left.)
- Read the written directions.
- Practice, practice, practice, and practice some more!

While you will probably need to look at the book occasionally, keep in mind that you will not be able to teach the verse effectively unless you can spend most of the time looking at your students.

HAND ALPHABET
(AND NUMBER 5)

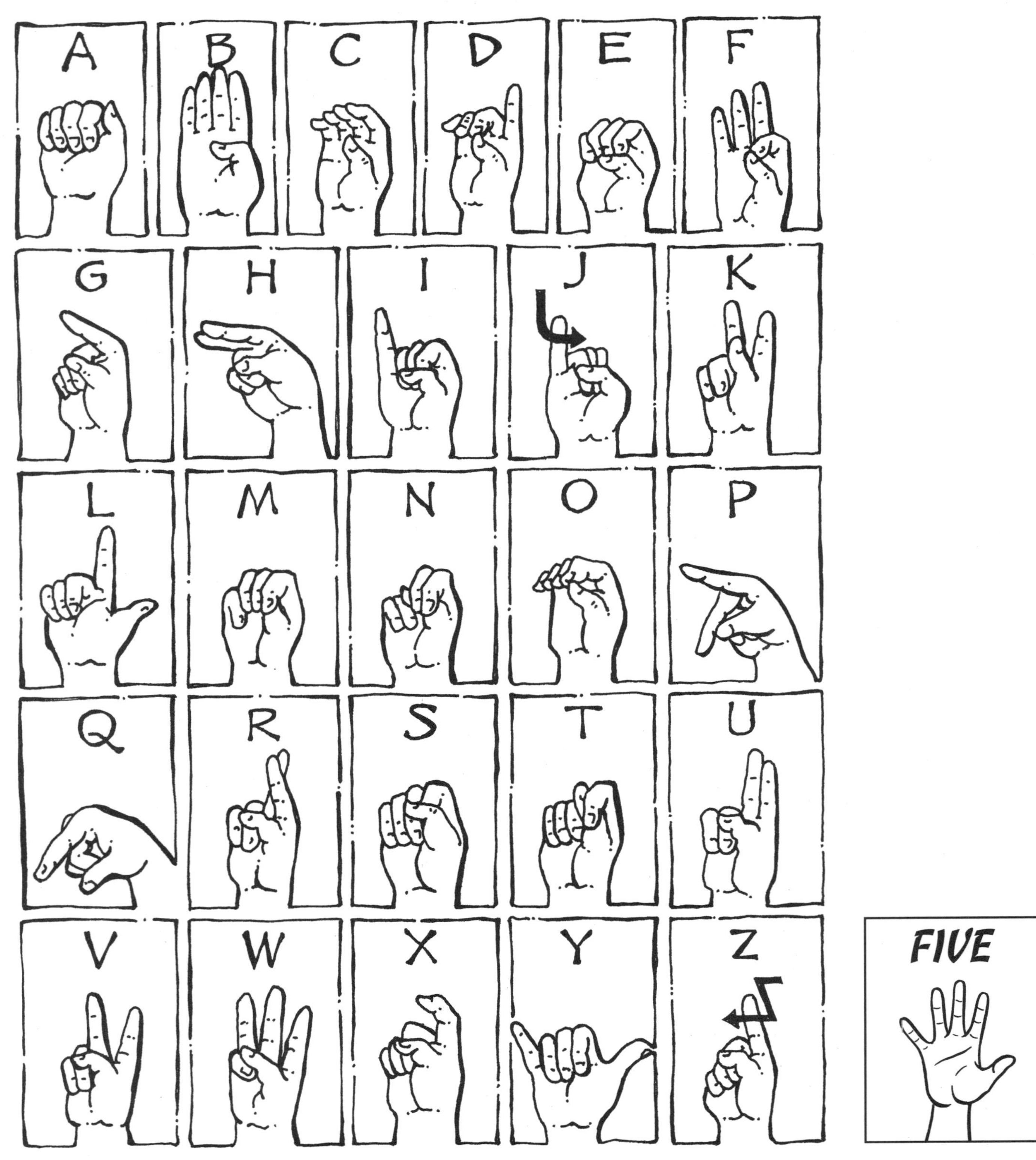

CONTENTS

Hear, O Israel: The LORD is our God, the LORD alone.

HEAR

Cup the right hand around the right ear.

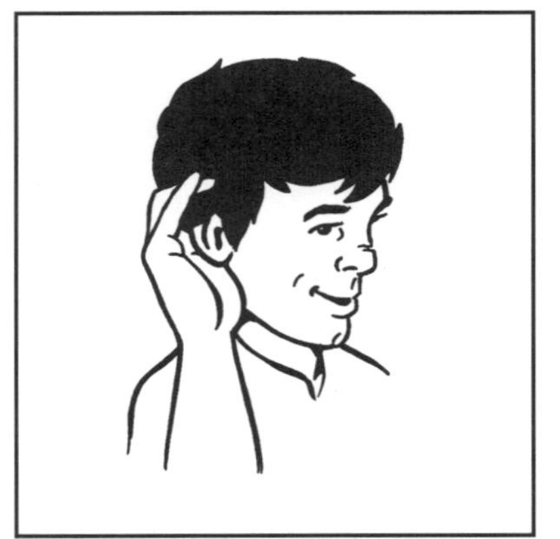

(O) ISRAEL

Hold the right hand in the "I" position, with the little finger extended and the palm toward the face. Pull the right hand down the left side of the face to the chin and then down the right side of face (this movement represents the outline of the traditional Jewish beard).

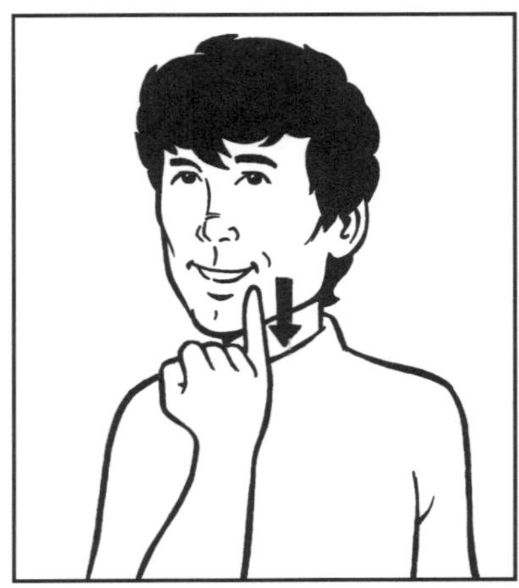

(THE) LORD

Hold the right "L" hand first at the left shoulder (palm facing left, index finger pointing up) and then down at the right hip (palm facing down).

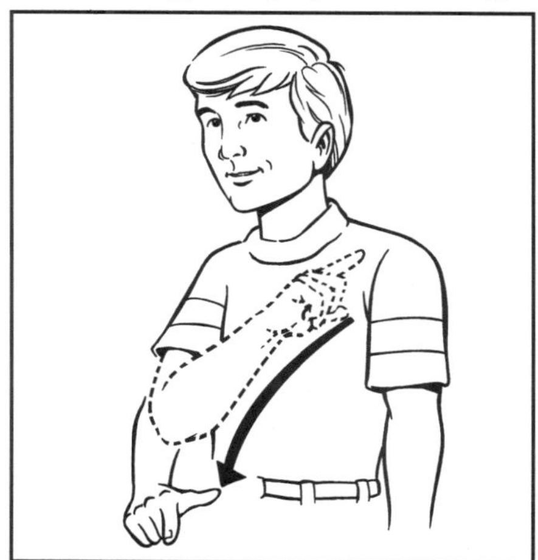

IS

Hold the tip of the right little finger to the lips, palm facing left. Move the hand straight out and away from the lips.

OUR

Make a "C" with the right hand, palm facing left, and hold it at the right shoulder. Swing the right hand across the chest to the left so that the palm faces inward.

GOD

Make a "G" with the right hand, palm facing left, and point forward and up at head level. Then move the right hand down and back toward the body, ending with an open palm facing left at chest level.

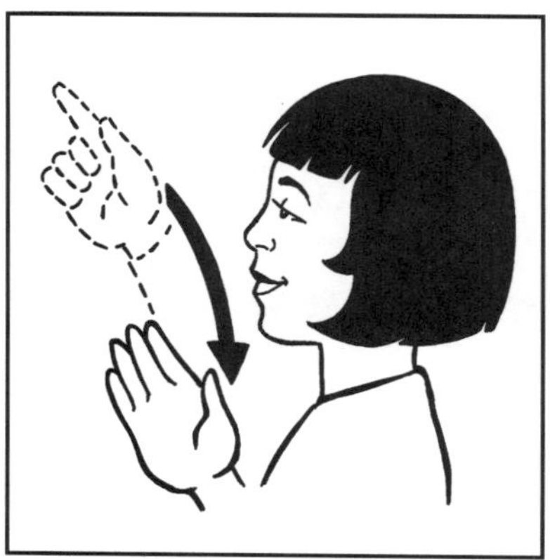

(THE) LORD

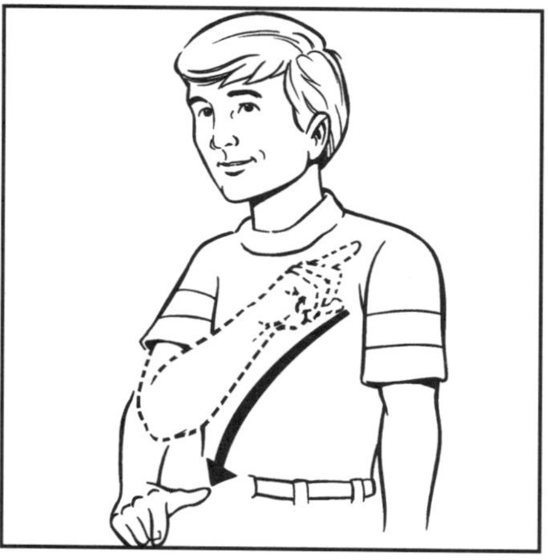

ALONE

With the right hand facing the body and the index finger extended and pointing up, make a counter-clockwise circle several times.

You shall love the LORD your God with all your heart, and with all your soul, and with all your might.

YOU

Point straight out in front with the right index finger.

SHALL

Place the right hand at ear level, with the palm facing the cheek. Move this hand forward.

LOVE

Cross both hands at the wrists and press them over the heart.

(THE) LORD

Hold the right "L" hand first at the left shoulder (palm facing left, index finger pointing up) and then down at the right hip (palm facing down).

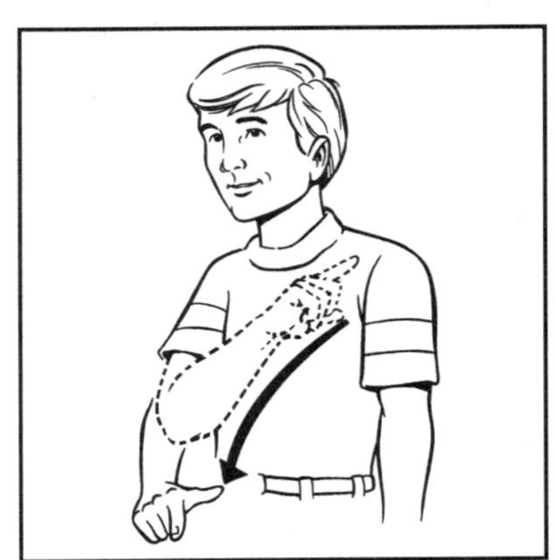

(YOUR) GOD

Make a "G" with the right hand, palm facing left, and point forward and up at head level. Then move the right hand down and back toward the body, ending with an open palm facing left at chest level.

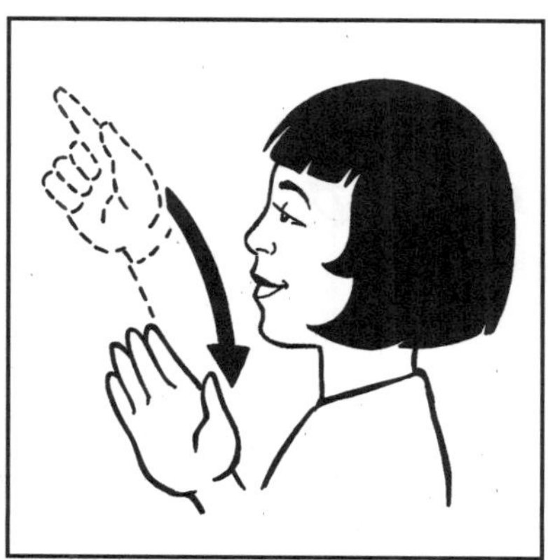

WITH

Bring the two "A" hands together with the palms facing.

ALL

Hold the left palm toward the body. Circle the right hand, palm facing out, out and around the left hand. End with the back of the right hand in the open left hand.

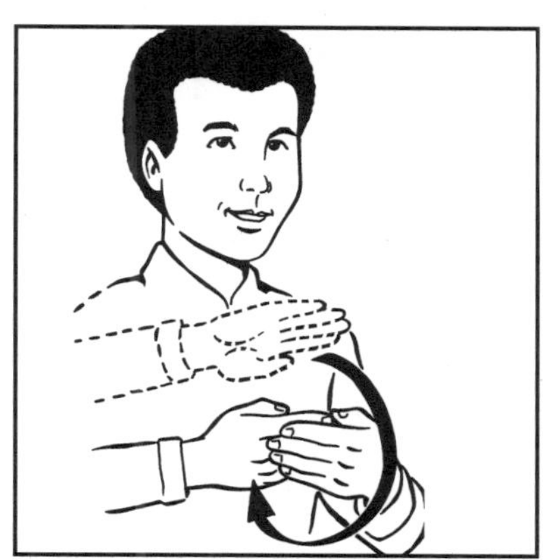

YOUR

Hold the right hand up with the fingers pointed up and palm facing out, and push it forward.

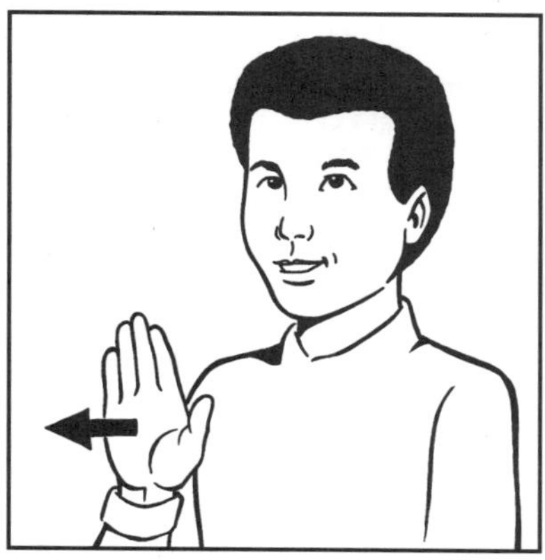

HEART

Use the index fingers to trace a heart shape on the chest.

AND

Hold the right hand out at chest level with the fingers slightly spread and the palm facing the left shoulder. Then pull the hand to the right while closing the fingers together.

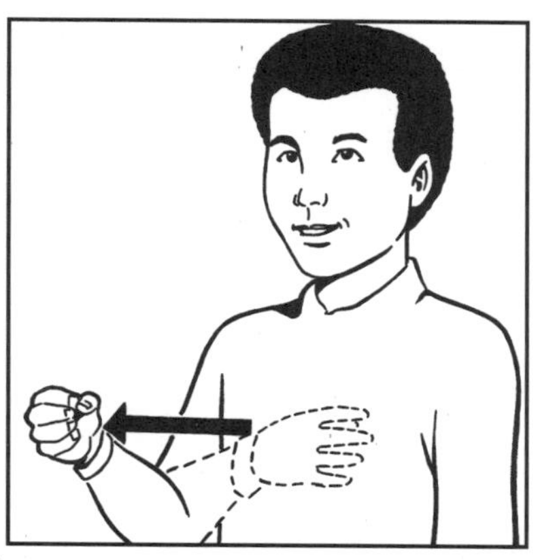

WITH

ALL

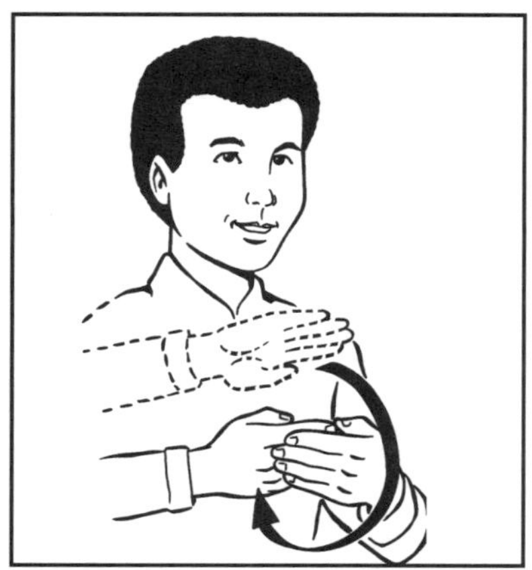

YOUR

SOUL

Pull the thumb and index finger of the right "F" hand, palm facing down, from inside the left "O" hand to up in front of the chest.

AND

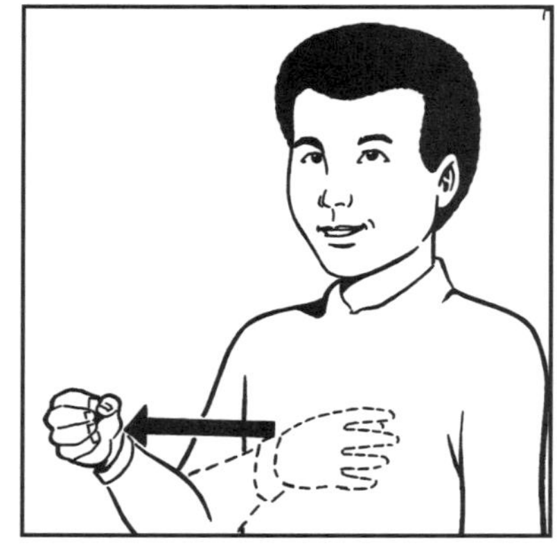

WITH

ALL

YOUR

MIGHT

Hold both hands in fists over the right side of the chest, then simultaneously move both fists up and out.

I was glad when they said to me, "Let us go to the house of the LORD!"

I

Hold the right "I" hand with the thumb against the chest and the palm facing left.

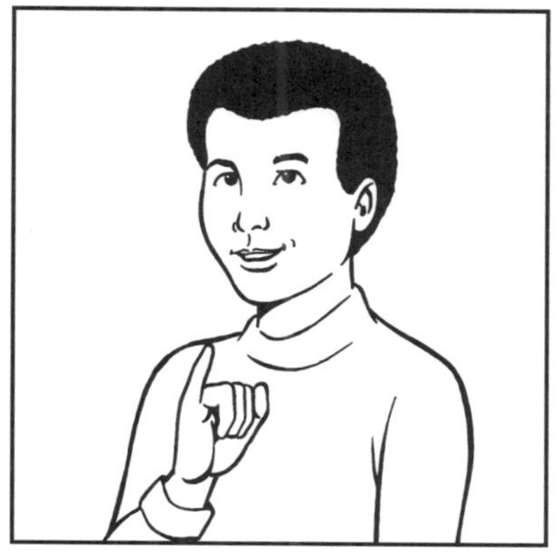

GLAD

Pat the chest several times with both hands (held open with palms on chest).

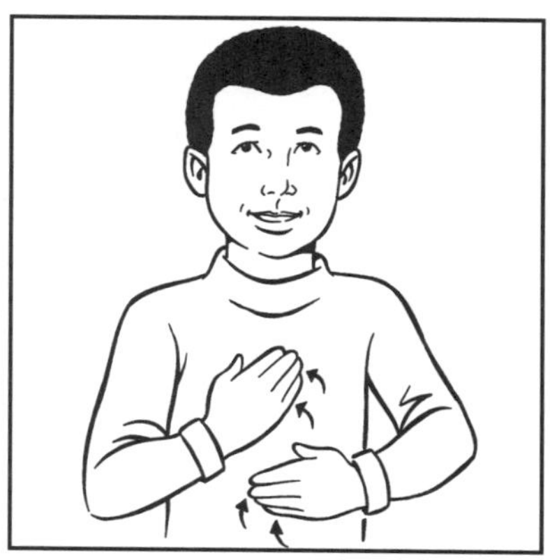

THEY

Point the right index finger forward, then move it across the body to the right.

WAS

Hold the right hand, palm facing the body, on the right side of the face. Move the hand back over the right shoulder.

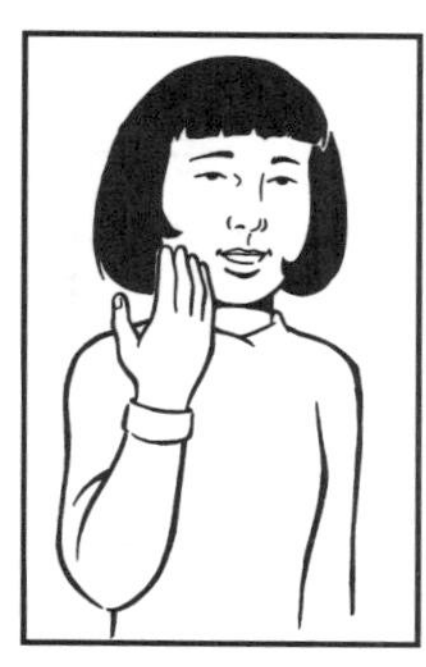

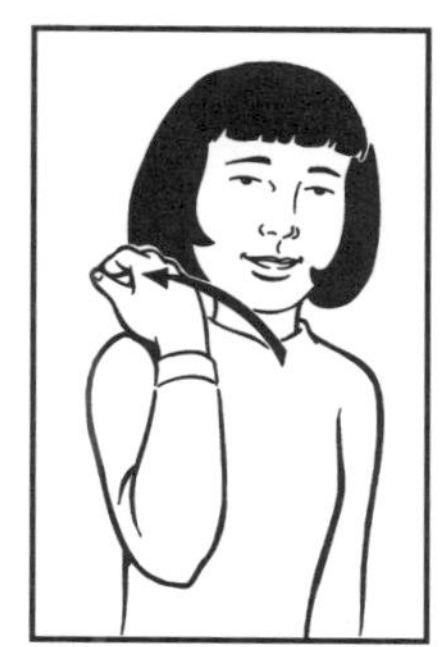

WHEN

Hold the right index finger above the left index finger and make a clockwise circle.

SAID

Hold the right index finger, palm facing down, in front of the mouth and then roll it forward and down.

TO

Point the right index finger to the left and move it forward slowly until it meets the tip of the left index finger, which is pointing up.

ME

Point the index finger of the right hand toward the chest.

LET

Hold both hands at chest level with palms facing each other and fingers pointing away from the body. Sweep both hands up and back toward the body so that the fingers are pointing up.

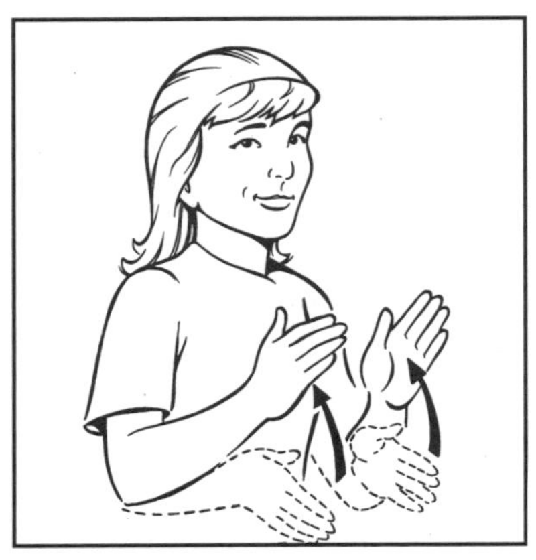

US

Hold the right hand in a "U" at the right shoulder, then curve the "U" right hand across the body to touch the left shoulder.

GO

Point the index fingers of both hands up, with one hand slightly behind the other. Then move both hands forward and down.

TO

(THE) HOUSE

Touch the fingertips of both hands together and then move the hands apart and down to outline the roof of a house.

OF

Use the right hand to spell the letters "O" and "F."

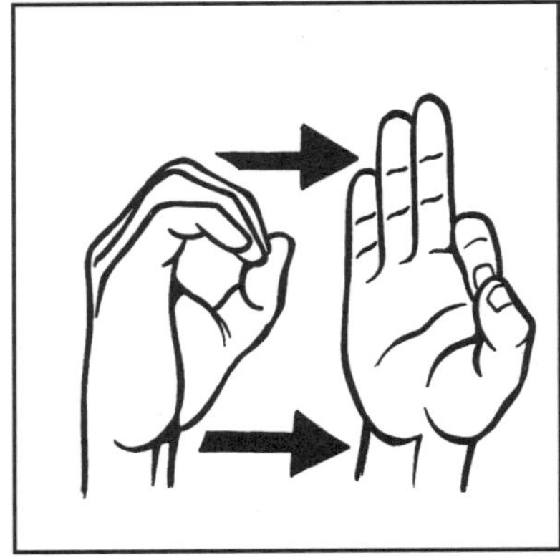

(THE) LORD

Hold the right "L" hand first at the left shoulder (palm facing left, index finger pointing up) and then down at the right hip (palm facing down).

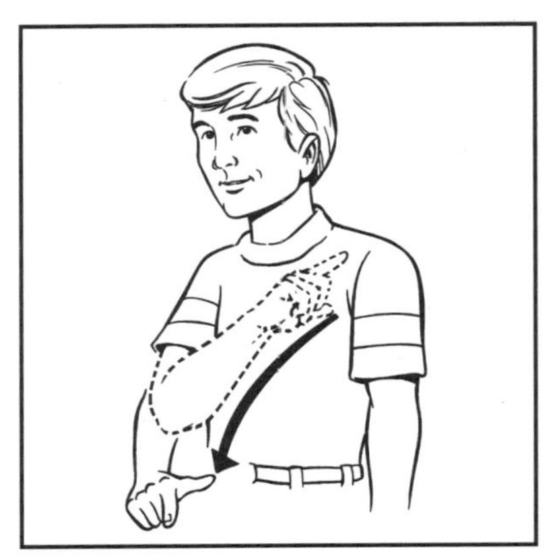

For everything there is a season,
and a time for every matter
under heaven.

FOR

Point the right index finger to the right temple, then point straight out in front of the face.

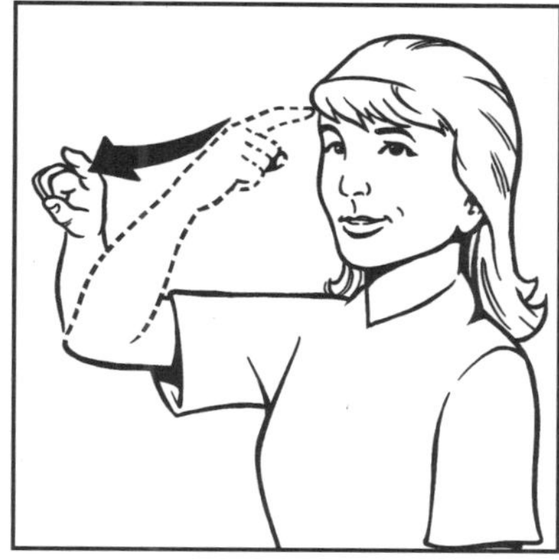

EVERY

Form an "A" with the left hand, palm facing right. Pull the knuckles of the right "A" hand repeatedly down the complete length of the left thumb toward the body.

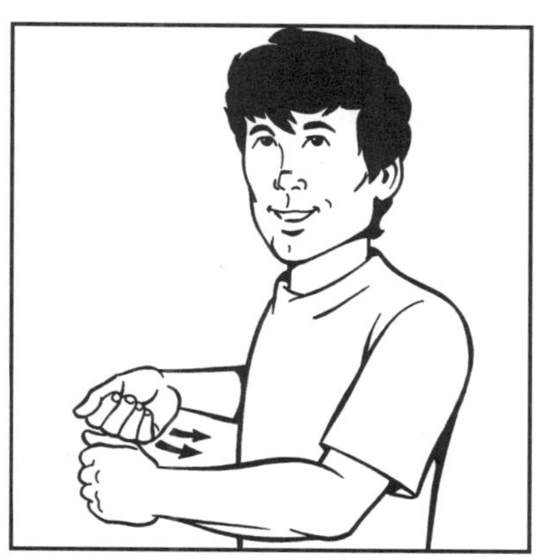

THING

Hold the right hand, palm up, outstretched in front of the chest. Drop the hand slightly and move it over to the right.

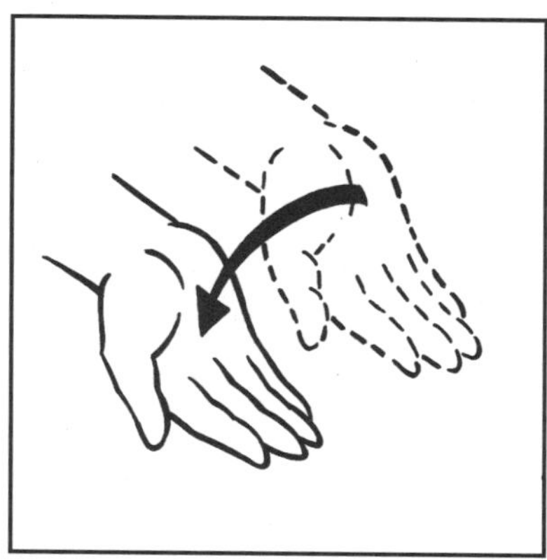

(THERE) IS

Hold the tip of the right little finger to the lips, palm facing left. Move the hand straight out and away from the lips.

(A) SEASON (OR TIME)

Make a "T" with the right hand, hold it against the left hand, palms facing, and make a clockwise circle.

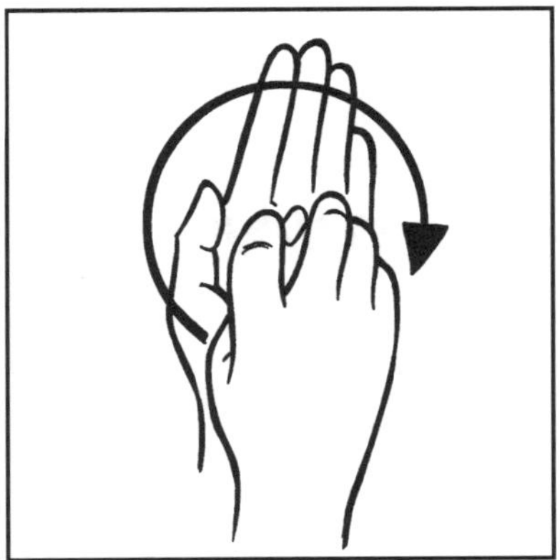

AND

Hold the right hand out at chest level with the fingers slightly spread and the palm facing the left shoulder. Then pull the hand to the right while closing the fingers together.

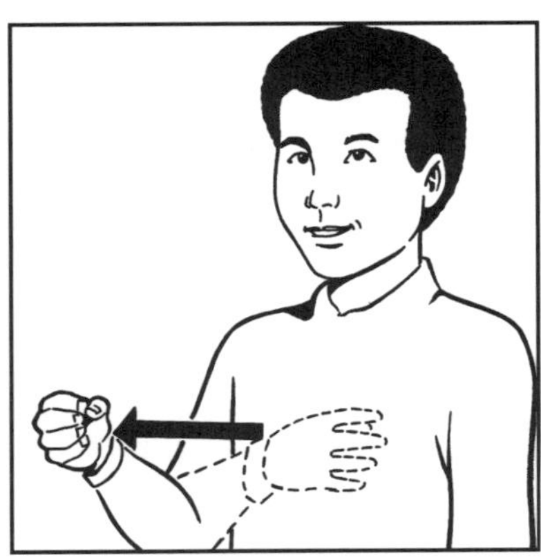

(A) TIME

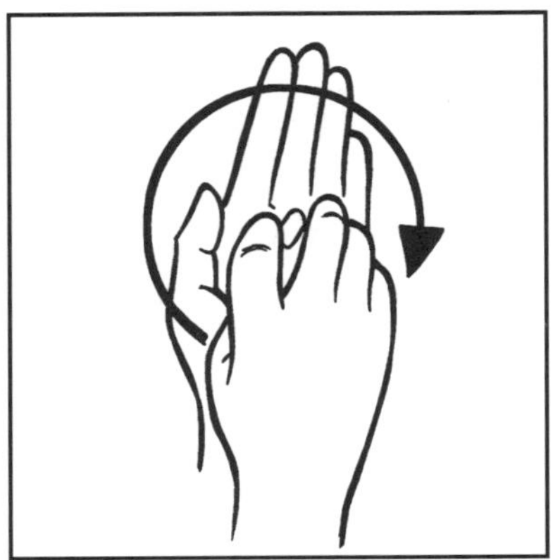

FOR

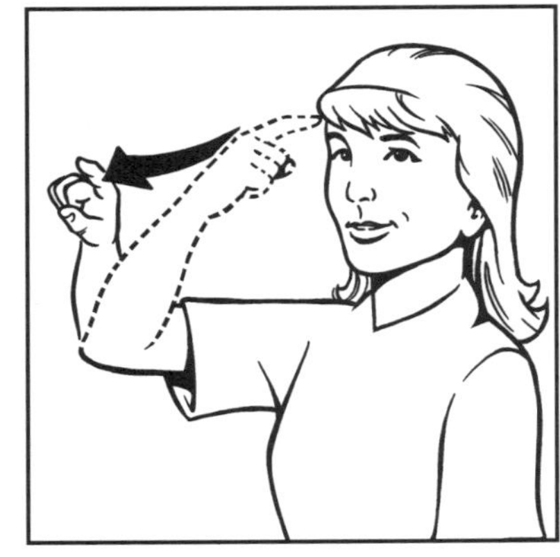

EVERY

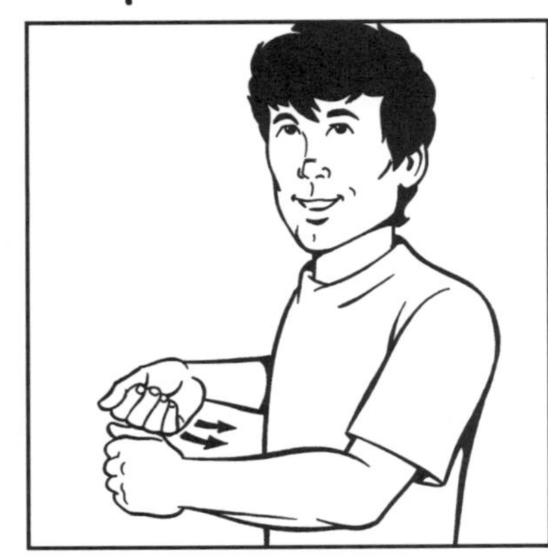

THING

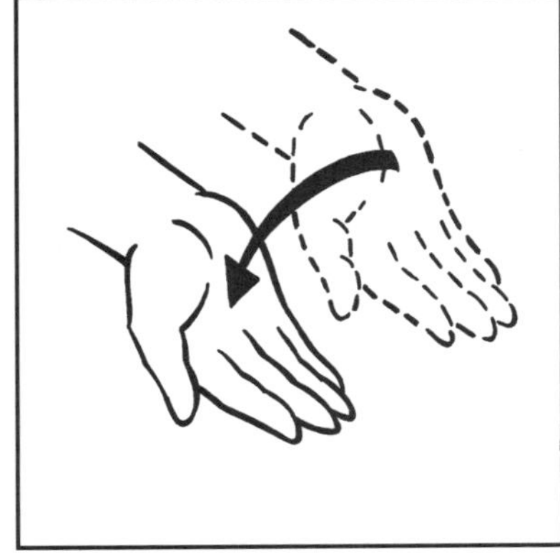

UNDER

Hold the right hand in the "A" position with the thumb pointing up and move it under the outstretched left hand.

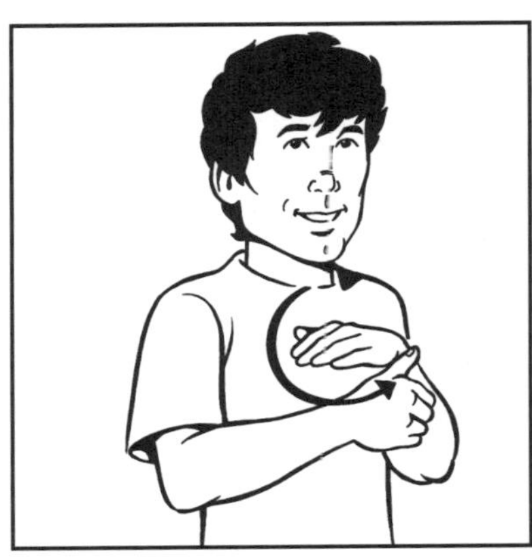

HEAVEN

Bend both arms at the elbows and hold both hands with fingers together pointing straight up. Then move both arms together in an arc. Just before the hands touch, move the right hand palm down so that it sweeps under the left hand and then up, ending with the palm of the right hand facing out.

For a child has been born for us, a son given to us;
authority rests upon his shoulders;
and he is named Wonderful Counselor,
Mighty God, Everlasting Father,
Prince of Peace.

(FOR A) CHILD (INFANT)

Hold both arms together as if holding a baby and rock them from side to side.

(HAS BEEN) BORN

Move the right hand, palm toward the body, so that it rests with its back against the left palm.

FOR

Point the right index finger to the right temple, then point straight out in front of the face.

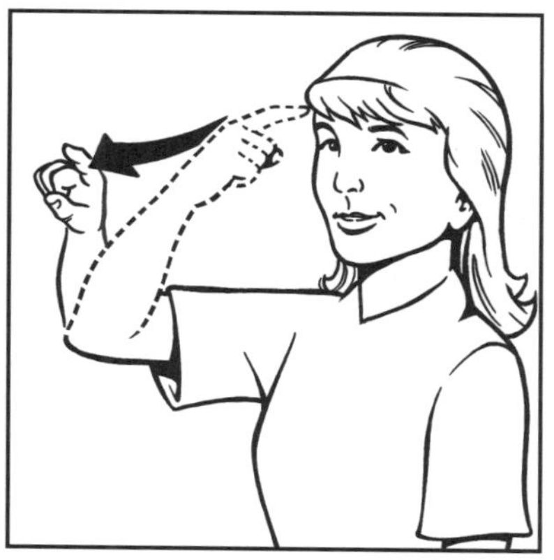

US

Hold the right hand in a "U" at the right shoulder, then curve the "U" right hand across the body to touch the left shoulder.

(A) SON

Bring the thumb and extended fingers of the right hand to the right side of the forehead to grasp an imaginary cap brim. Then rock the arms together in the sign for "child."

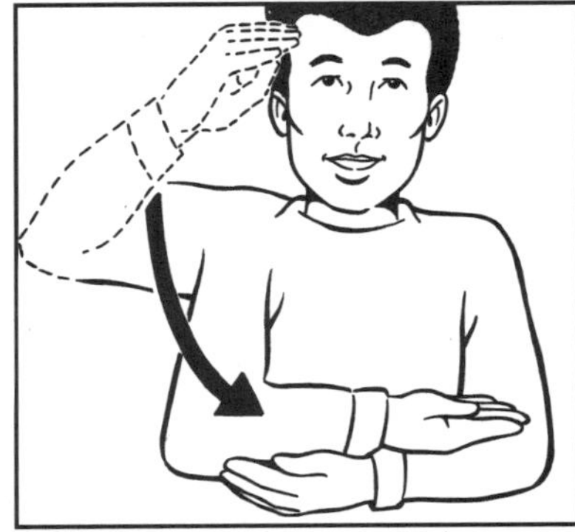

GIVEN

Hold both hands in front of the body, palms up and fingers and thumb touching on each hand. Then pull the hands in to the chest.

TO

Point the right index finger to the left and move it forward slowly until it meets the tip of the left index finger, which is pointing up.

US

AUTHORITY

Extend the left arm with the elbow bent. Move the right "A" hand in an arc from the left shoulder to the inside of the left elbow.

RESTS (18)

Hold the tip of the right little finger to the lips, palm facing left. Move the hand straight out and away from the lips.

UPON

Place the right hand, palm down, on the back of the left hand.

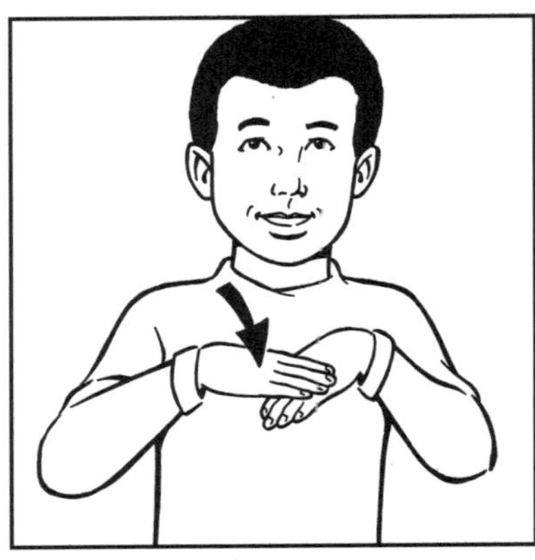

HIS

Hold the right hand against the forehead as if saluting. Then lower the right hand to the right shoulder, keeping the open palm facing out, and move the hand straight forward.

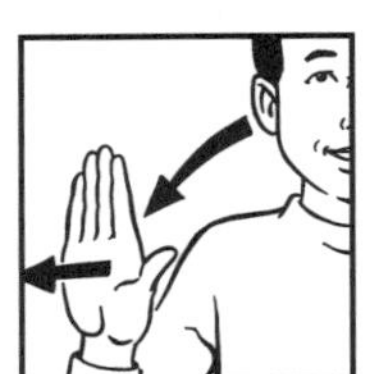

SHOULDERS

Place both hands on the right shoulder.

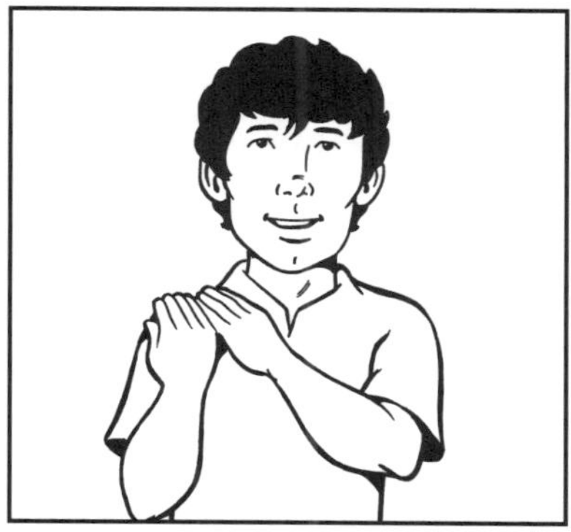

AND

Hold the right hand out at chest level with the fingers slightly spread and the palm facing the left shoulder. Then pull the hand to the right while closing the fingers together.

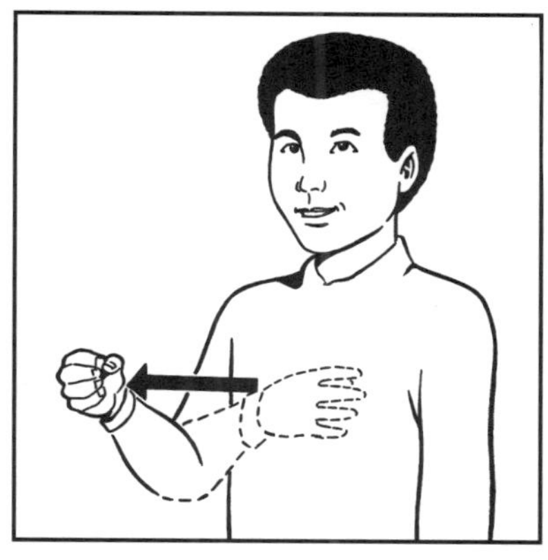

HE (THY)

Raise the right hand in the "5" position on the right side of the head, with the palm facing out. Move the hand up and away, toward heaven.

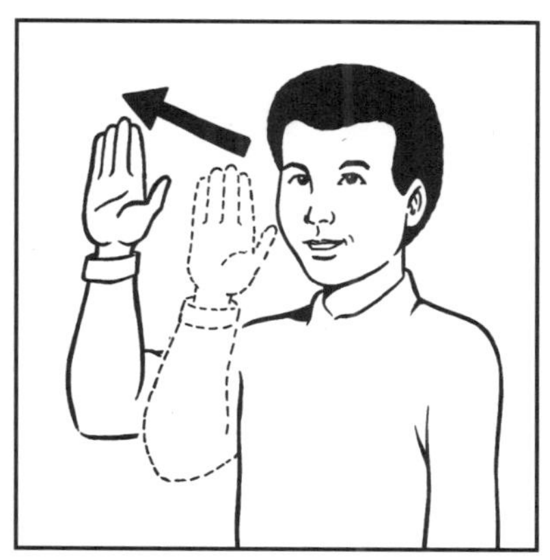

IS

NAMED

Both hands make an "H" and the index fingers cross, right hand on top, to form an x-shape. Move both hands forward, away from the body.

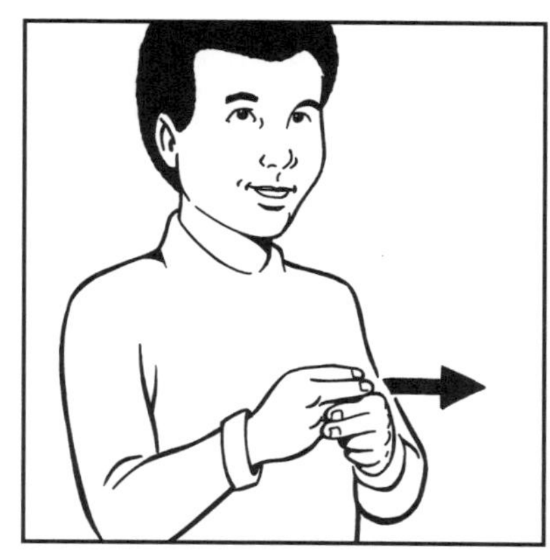

WONDERFUL

With arms raised, hands open, and all fingers outstretched, pat the air repeatedly.

COUNSELOR

Hold the left hand palm down in front of the body. Place the fingers of the right hand on top of the left hand, move them down the left hand away from the body, then open the right hand above the left hand, keeping the palm open and the right thumb on the back of the left hand. Then hold both hands, palms facing each other, at the sides and simultaneously move them down to hip level.

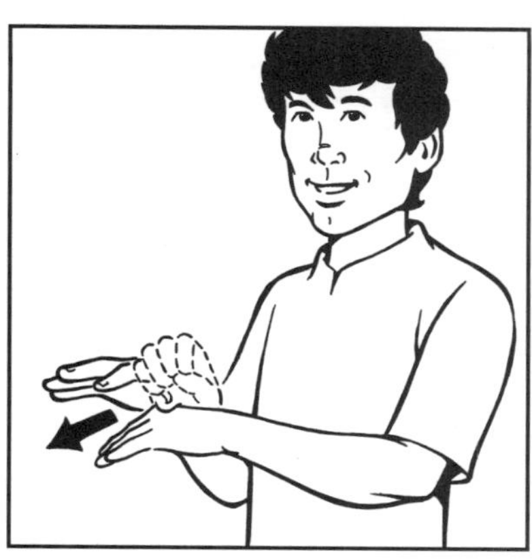

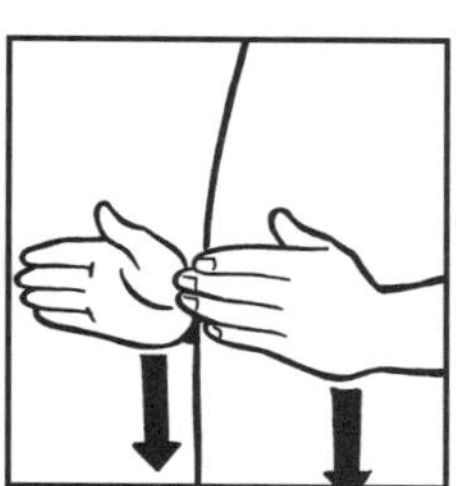

MIGHTY (AUTHORITY)

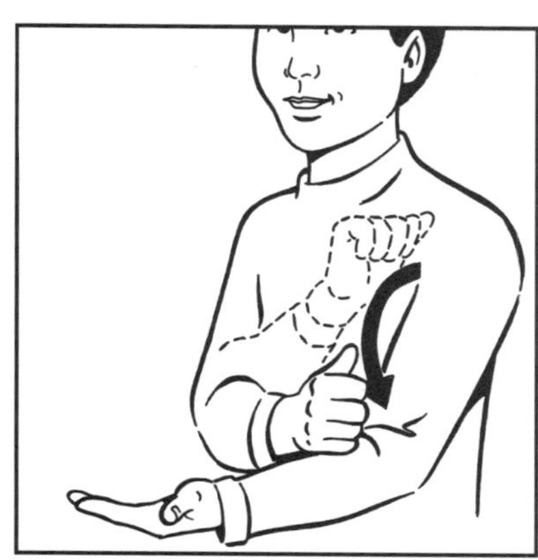

GOD

Make a "G" with the right hand, palm facing left, and point forward and up at head level. Then move the right hand down and back toward the body, ending with an open palm facing left at chest level.

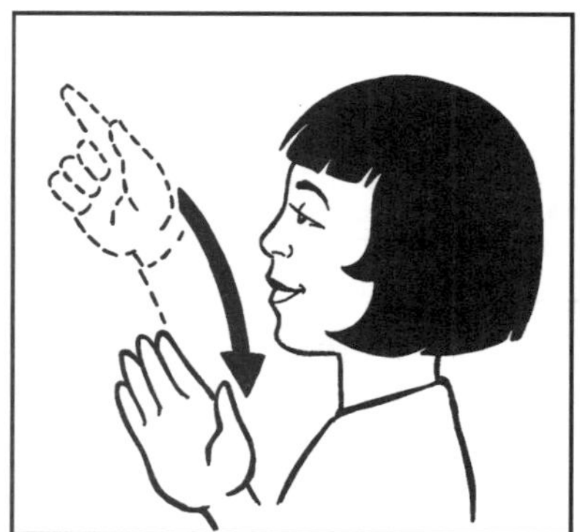

EVERLASTING (ETERNAL)

With the right hand held palm up, use the right index finger to trace a clockwise circle in the air. Then, with the right hand palm down in the "Y" position, move the hand straight forward.

FATHER

Place the right "A" hand at the forehead with the palm facing left and place the left "A" hand out in front of the forehead with the palm facing right. Move both hands upward and outward toward the left while opening both hands into the "5" position.

PRINCE

Form the letter "P" with the right hand at the left shoulder, then move the right hand across the chest to the right.

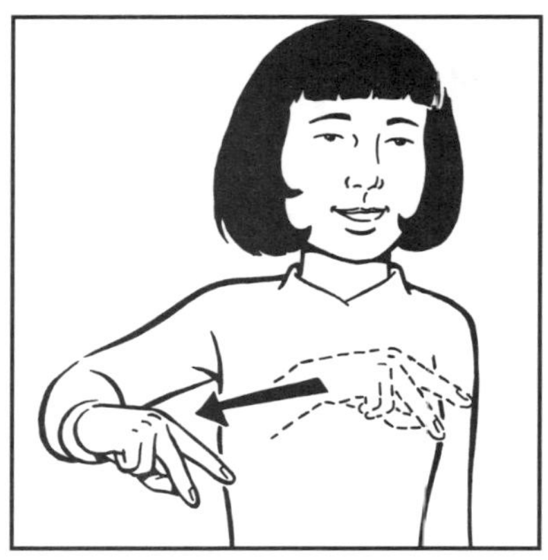

OF

Use the right hand to spell the letters "O" and "F."

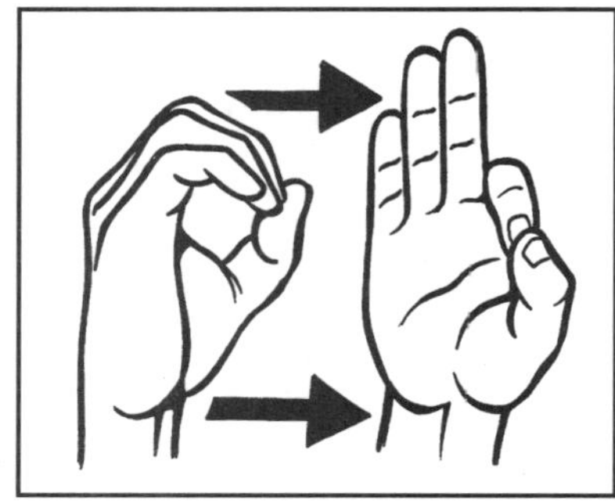

PEACE

Hold both hands palm to palm, with the right hand resting in the left hand, at the left shoulder. Rotate hands to the left so that the left hand is on top. Then both hands, palms down, separate and move down and to the sides in a smooth, continuous movement.

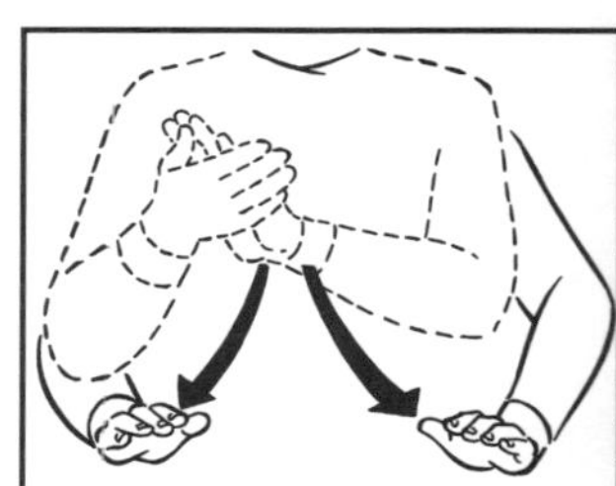

THE LORD'S PRAYER

Our Father, who art in heaven,
hallowed be thy name.
Thy kingdom come,
thy will be done on earth
as it is in heaven.
Give us this day our daily bread.
And forgive us our trespasses,
as we forgive those who trespass against us.
And lead us not into temptation,
but deliver us from evil.
For thine is the kingdom,
and the power, and the glory, forever.
Amen.

OUR

Make a "C" with the right hand, palm facing left, and hold it at the right shoulder. Swing the right hand across the chest to the left so that the palm faces inward.

FATHER (HEAVENLY FATHER)

Place the right "A" hand at the forehead with the palm facing left and place the left "A" hand out in front of the forehead with the palm facing right. Move both hands upward and outward toward the left while opening both hands into the "5" position.

WHO

Make a small counterclockwise circle with the right index finger in front of pursed lips.

ART (IS)

Hold the tip of the right little finger to the lips, palm facing left. Move the hand straight out and away from the lips.

IN

Move the fingers of the left hand down into the right hand.

HEAVEN

Bend both arms at the elbows and hold both hands with fingers together pointing straight up. Then move both arms together in an arc. Just before the hands touch, move the right hand palm down so that it sweeps under the left hand and then up, ending with the palm of the right hand facing out.

HALLOWED (HOLY)

Form an "H" with the right hand and make a circle over the upturned left palm. Then move the right hand across the left palm, moving from the wrist to the fingertips.

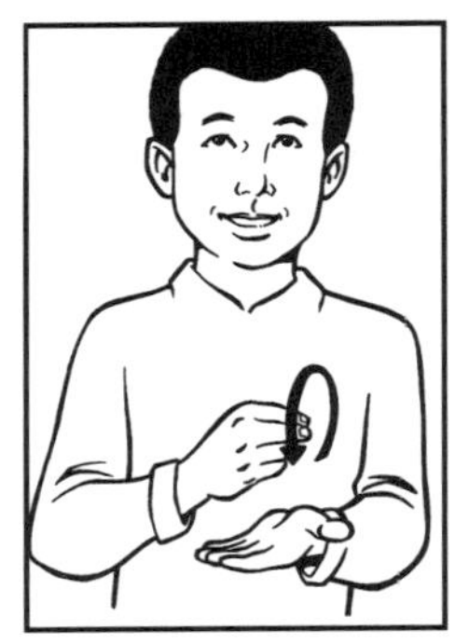

BE

Touch the "B" right hand to the lips and move it straight forward, away from the body.

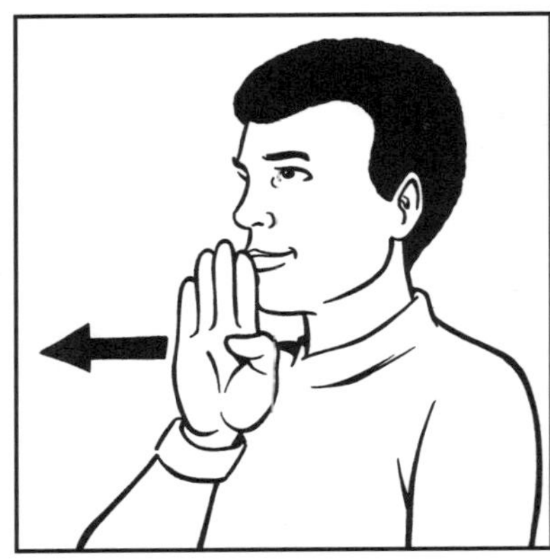

THY (YOUR)

Raise the right hand in the "5" position on the right side of the head, with the palm facing out. Move the hand up and away, toward heaven.

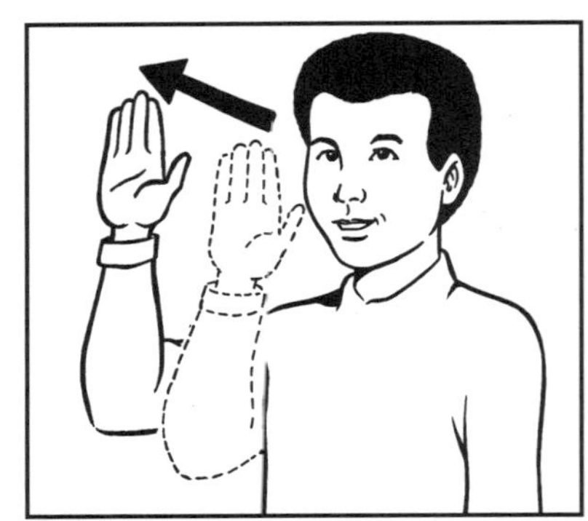

NAME
Both hands make an "H" and the index fingers cross, right hand on top, to form an x-shape.

THY (YOUR)

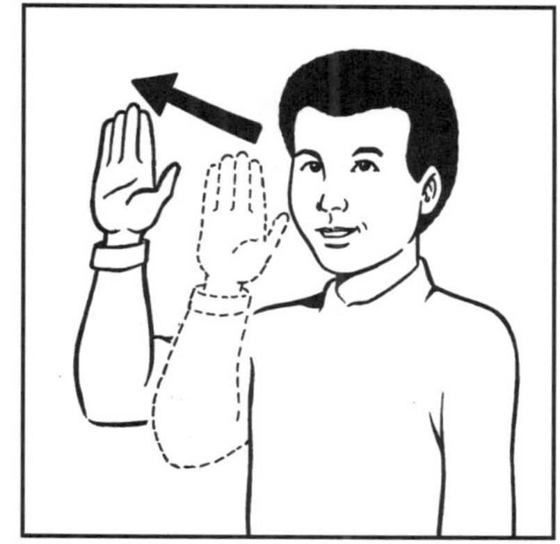

KINGDOM
Move the right "K" hand, palm facing left, from the left shoulder down to the right hip. Then open the right hand, palm facing down, and move it upward in an arc to circle over the downturned left hand.

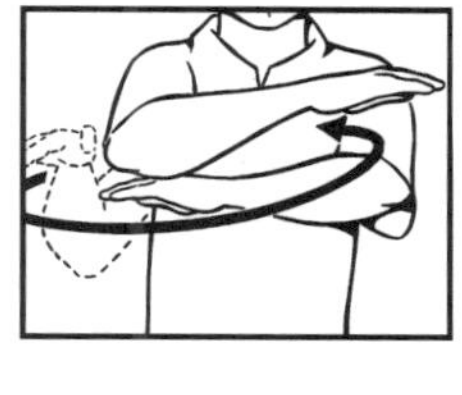

COME
Raise both hands in the "G" position above the head with the palms facing inward. Then move both hands down until they point inward toward the chest.

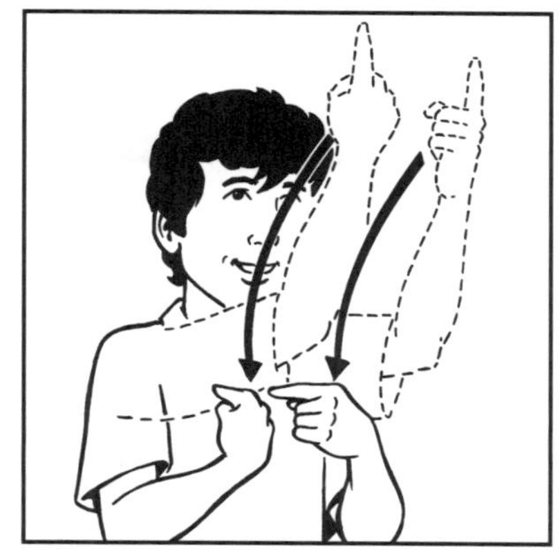

THY (YOUR)

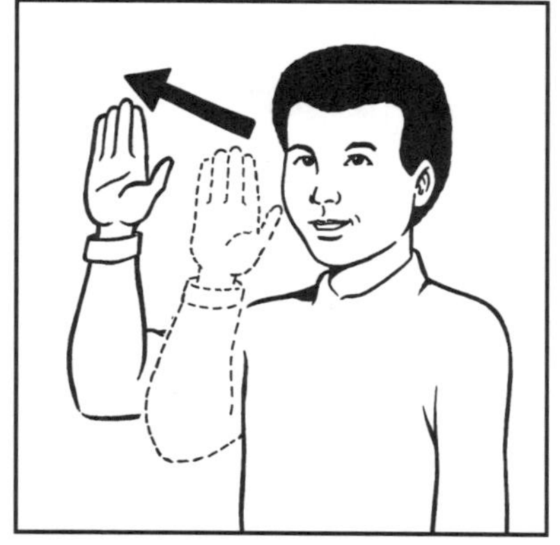

WILL
Hold both hands side by side with the palms turned up and the fingers slightly curled. Then quickly close the fingers in a grasping motion while moving both hands in toward the body.

(BE) DONE
With both hands open and palms down, swing the hands from right to left.

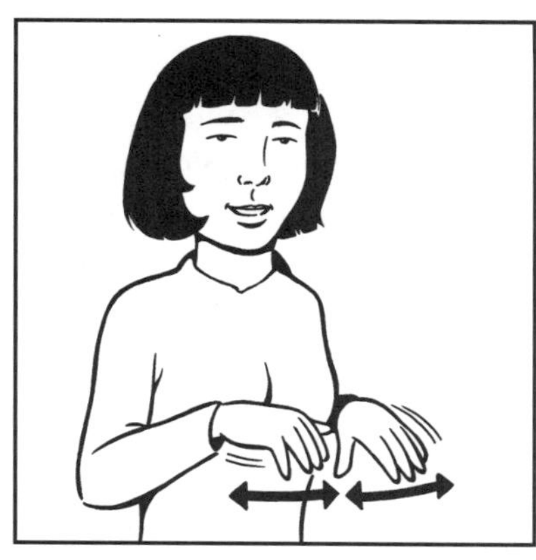

ON
Place the fingers of the right hand on the back of the left hand, palm facing down.

EARTH
With the left hand make an "S," and grip it with the thumb and middle finger of the right hand; then rock the left hand from side to side.

AS

Hold both index fingers, pointing forward and palms facing down, together to the left. Bring the fingers together. Then move both fingers to the other side of the body while separating the fingers an inch or two and then bring them together again.

(IT) IS

IN

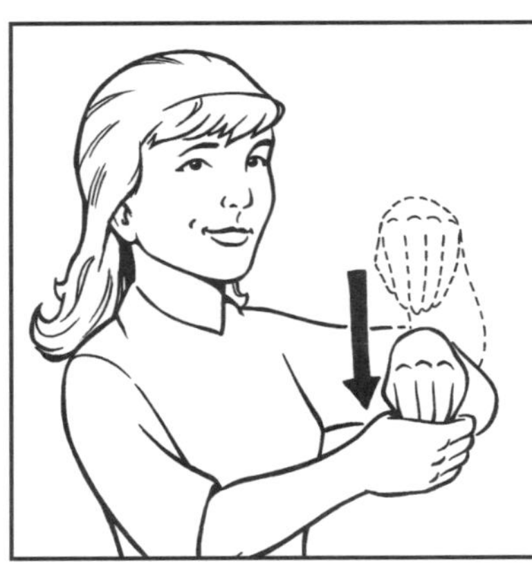

HEAVEN

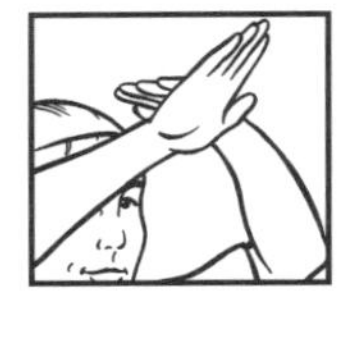

GIVE

Hold both hands in front of the body, palms up and fingers and thumb touching on each hand. Then pull the hands in to the chest.

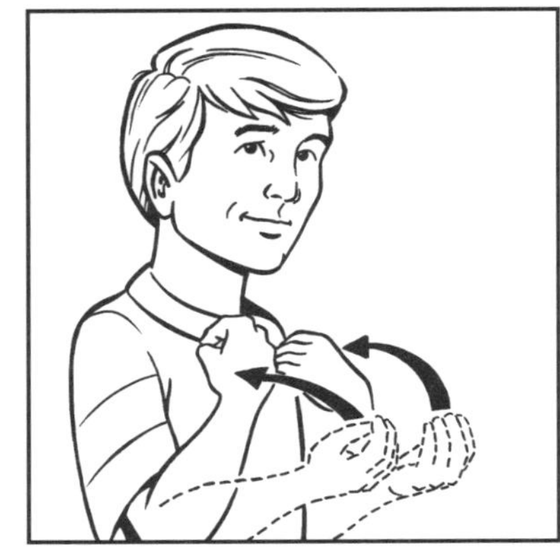

US

Hold the right hand in a "U" at the right shoulder, then curve the "U" right hand across the body to touch the left shoulder.

THIS

Hold both hands palm up, then lower them slightly.

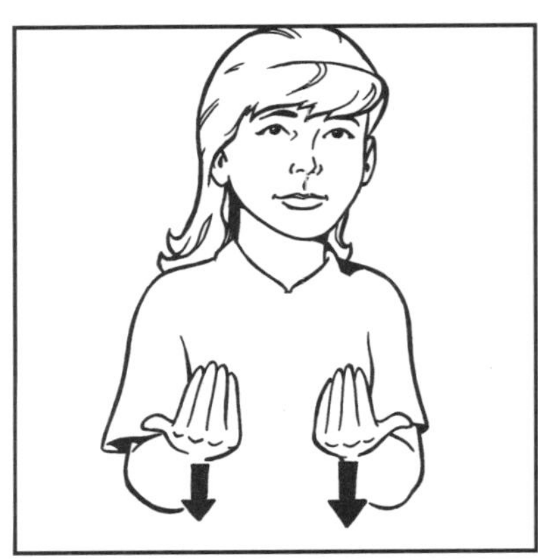

DAY

Hold the left arm palm down across the front of the body. Form the letter "D," palm facing left and index finger pointing up, with the right hand and rest the right elbow on the back of the left hand. Move the right arm in an arc until the index finger points to the crook of the left elbow.

OUR

DAILY

With the right hand, make a fist with the thumb out and rub it from the cheek to the chin several times.

BREAD

Hold the left hand in front of the body. Move the little finger side of the right hand across the left hand as if slicing bread.

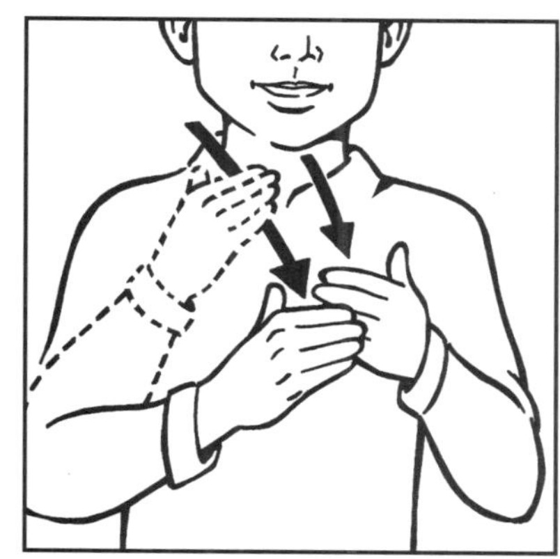

AND

Hold the right hand out at chest level with the fingers slightly spread and the palm facing the left shoulder. Then pull the hand to the right while closing the fingers together.

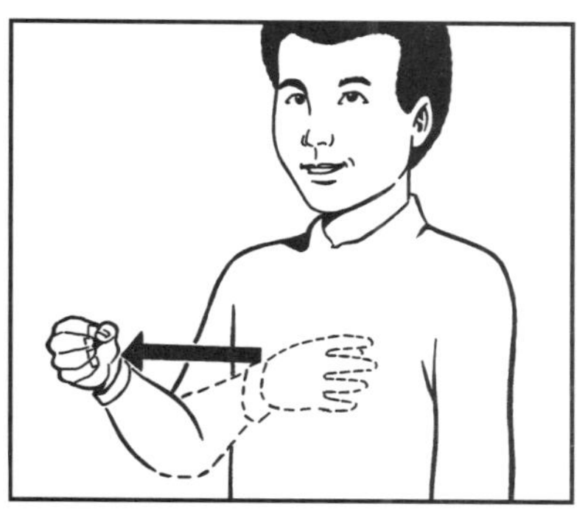

FORGIVE

Stroke the lower part of the left-hand palm with the right fingertips several times.

US

OUR

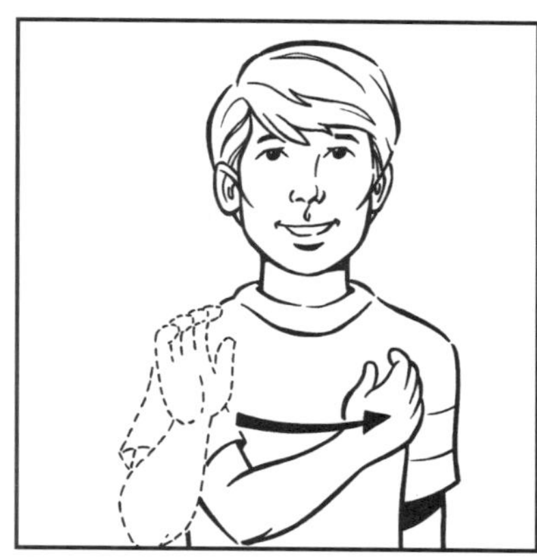

TRESPASSES

Point both index fingers toward each other with palms facing toward the body. Move the fingers simultaneously toward each other and closer to the body.

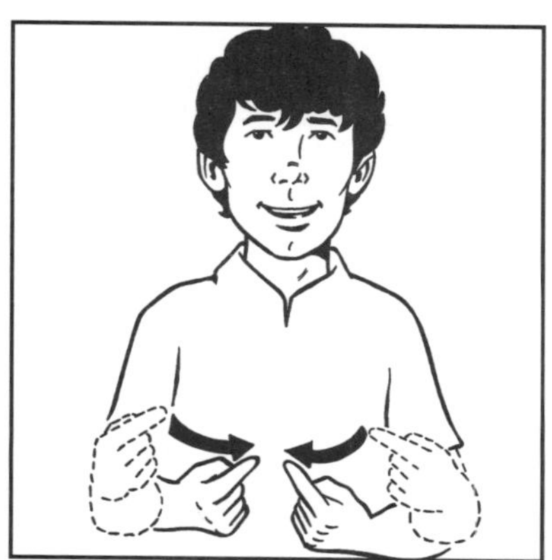

AS

WE

Point the right index finger to the right shoulder and then swing it across to the left shoulder.

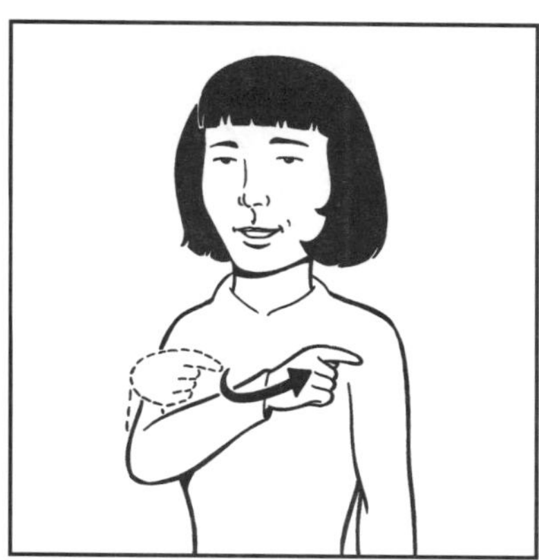

FORGIVE

THOSE

Point the right index finger straight out in front, then move the finger in one sweeping motion to the left.

WHO

TRESPASS

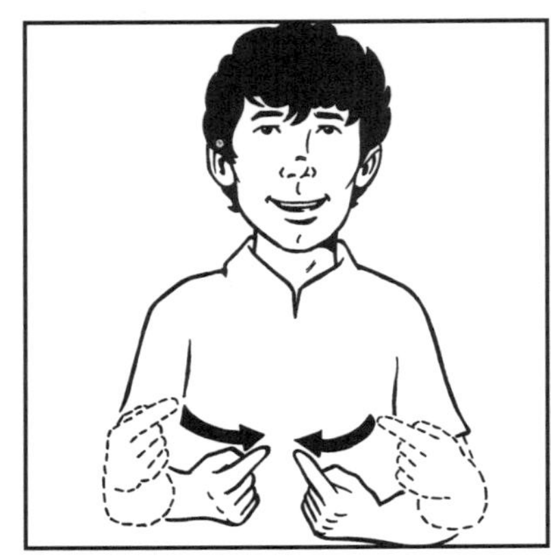

AGAINST

Hold the left hand with the fingers pointing up and the palm facing right. Thrust the fingers of the right hand, palm facing inward, into the open left palm.

US

AND

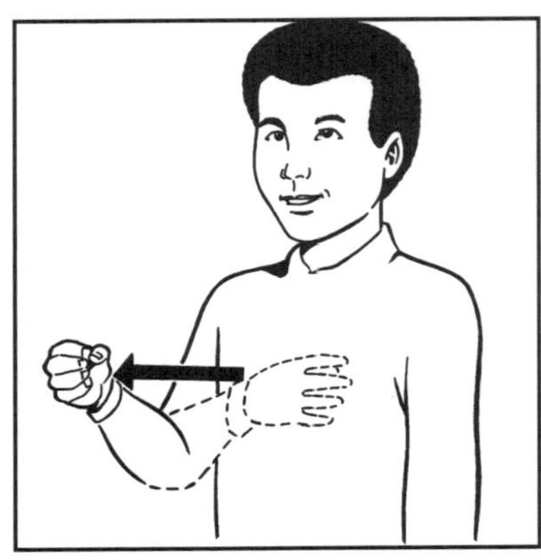

LEAD

With the right hand, grasp the tips of the left fingers and pull the left hand forward.

US

NOT

Place the right "A" hand under the chin. Move the thumb forward while moving the head from side to side, indicating "no."

INTO

Move the right hand down toward, behind, and under the left hand.

TEMPTATION

Tap the elbow of the bent left arm with the right index finger.

BUT

Cross the index fingers of both hands in front of the body, then pull the hands apart.

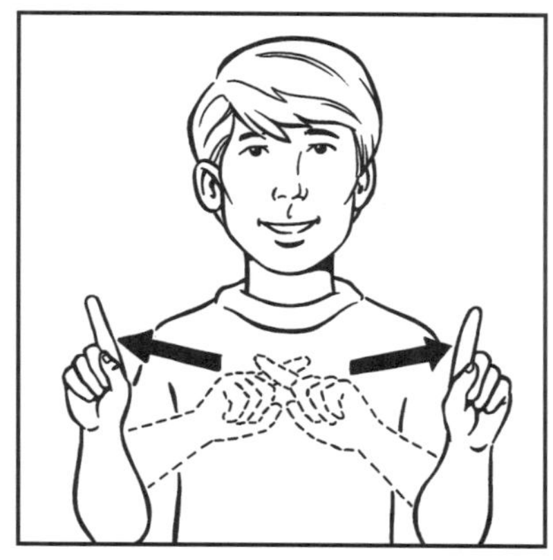

DELIVER

Cross both hands in front of the body as if bound at the wrists. Twist the wrists away from each other, ending with the palms facing forward in front of each shoulder.

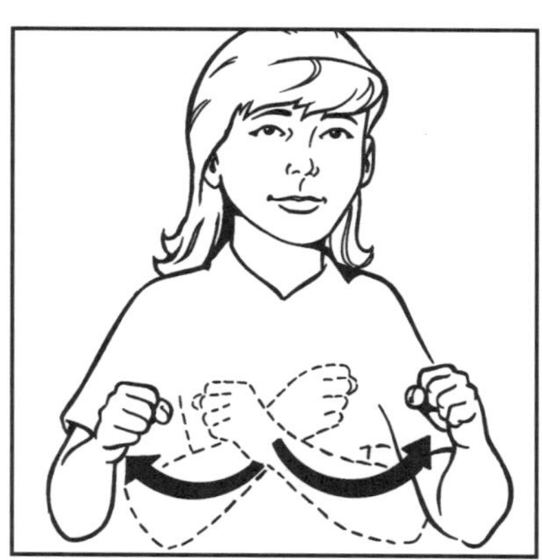

US

FROM

With index fingers crooked, point both hands away from the body. Place the knuckle of the right index finger on the base of the left index finger and then move the right hand up and away in a slight curve toward the body.

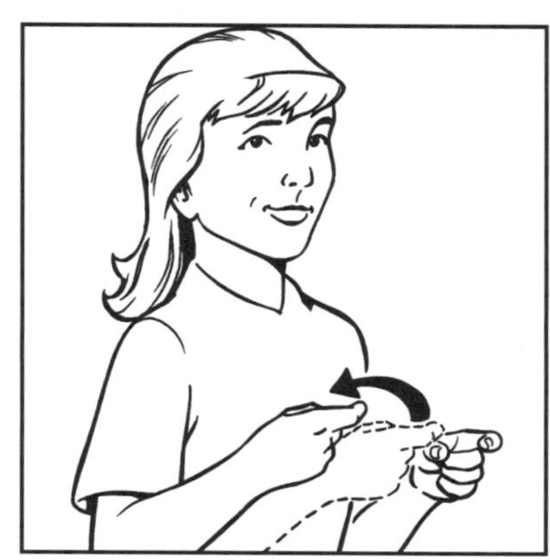

EVIL (TRESPASS)

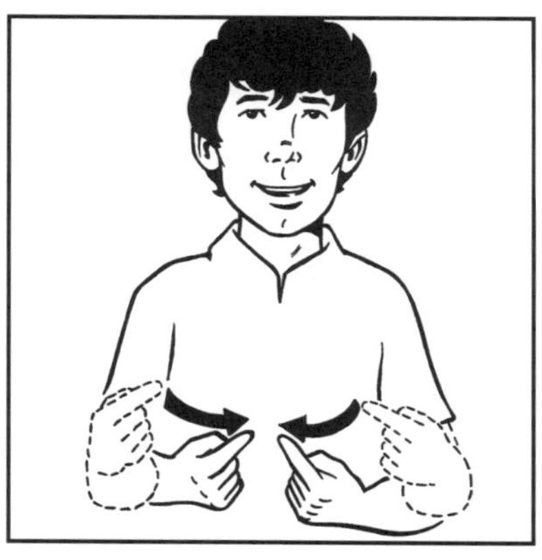

FOR

Point the right index finger to the right temple, then point straight out in front of the face.

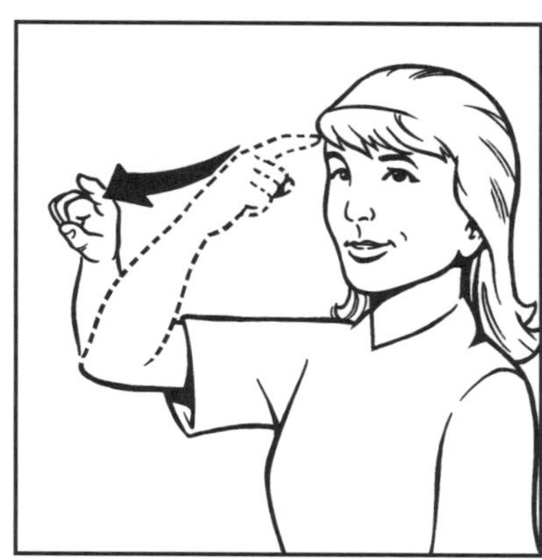

THINE (YOURS)

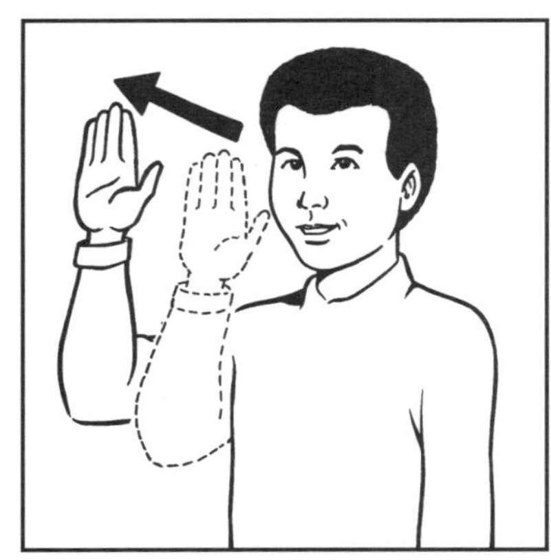

IS

(THE) KINGDOM

 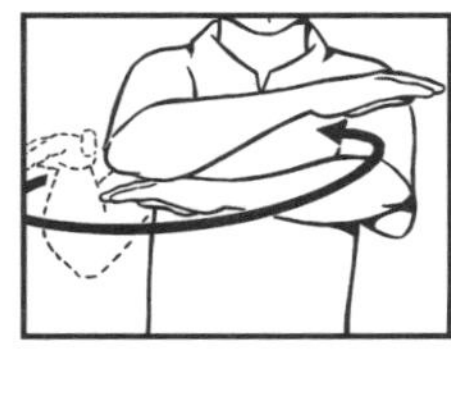

AND

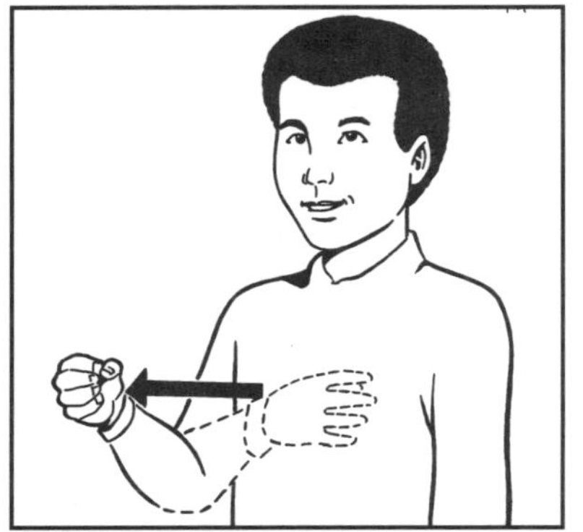

(THE) POWER

With both hands in the "S" position facing the body, move them from in front of the right side of the chest outward toward the left with force.

AND

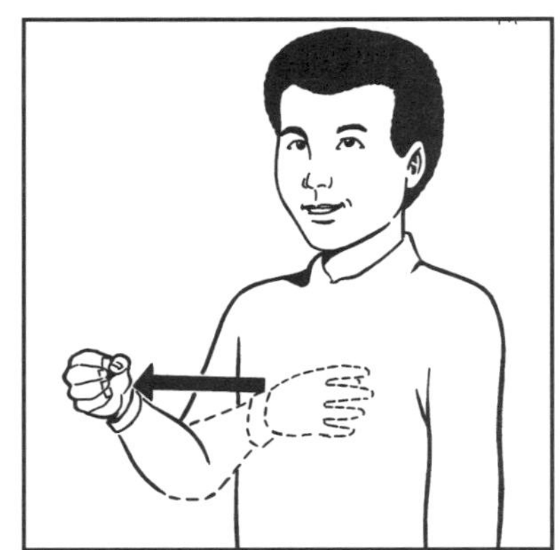

(THE) GLORY

Begin by holding the right hand over the upturned left palm. Then bring the right hand up above the shoulder, opening into a "5" hand and wiggling the fingers as the hand moves.

FOREVER

First point the right index finger to the forehead, then move it forward to trace a clockwise circle in the air. Then form a "Y" and move the hand forward and up.

AMEN

Hold the left hand palm up in front of the body. Hold the right "A" hand in front of the body, knuckles down, then move it to the left until it rests in the left palm with the knuckles facing left.

I am bringing you
good news of great joy
for all the people:
to you is born this day
in the city of David a Savior,
who is the Messiah,
the Lord.

I

Hold the right "I" hand with the thumb against the chest and the palm facing left.

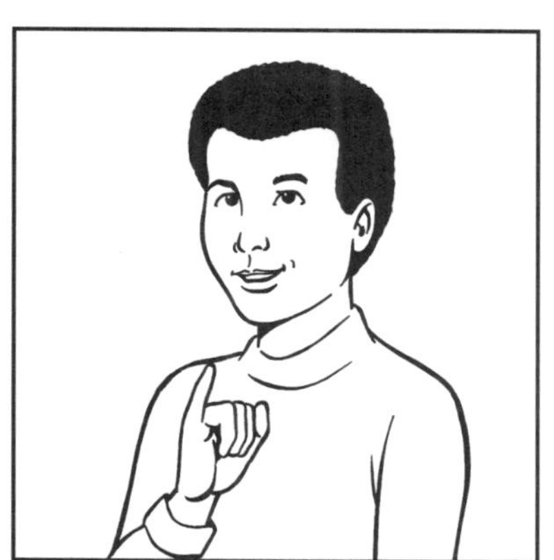

(AM) BRINGING

Hold both hands, palms up, in front of the chest. Move both hands together in an arc to the right.

YOU

Point straight out in front with the right index finger.

GOOD

Touch the fingers of the right hand to the lips. Then move the right hand down and place it palm up in the left hand.

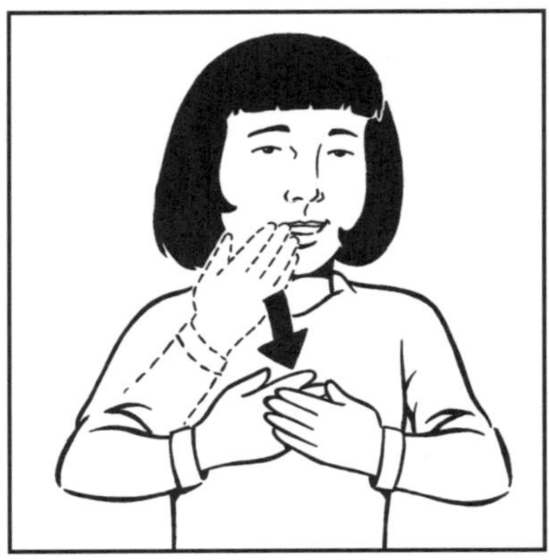

NEWS

Hold both hands at the forehead, fingertips and thumbs of each hand touching. Move both hands down and away, ending the motion with both palms open and facing up.

OF

Use the right hand to spell the letters "O" and "F."

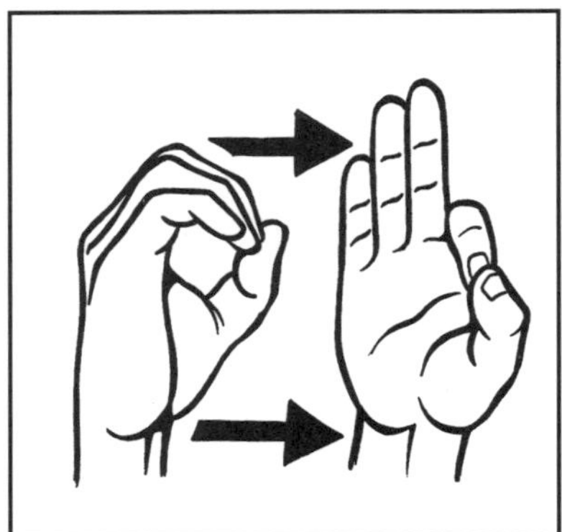

GREAT (WONDERFUL)

With arms raised and hands in a "5," pat the air repeatedly.

JOY

Both hands, with palms facing the chest, move in alternating circles away from the body.

FOR

Point the right index finger to the right temple, then point straight out in front of the face.

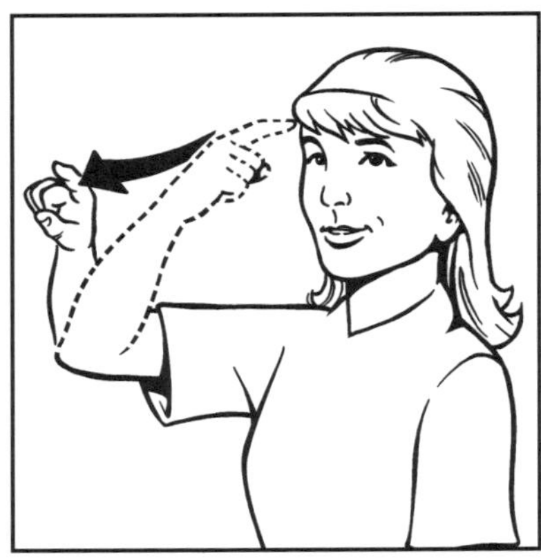

ALL

Hold the left palm facing the body. Circle the right hand, palm facing out, out and around the left hand, and end with the back of the right hand in the open left hand.

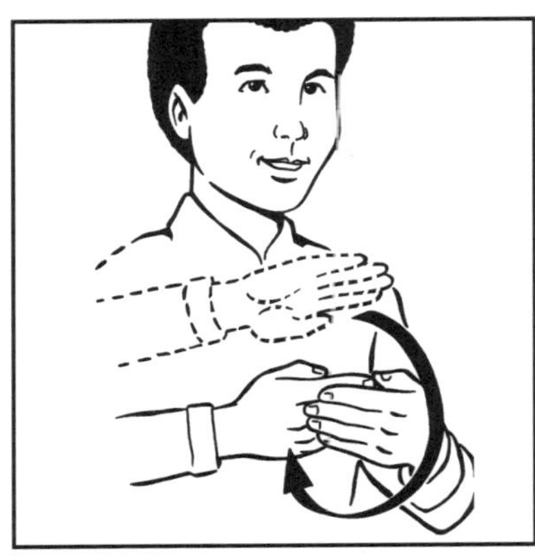

(THE) PEOPLE

Both "P" hands point forward and move down and away from each other.

TO

Point the right index finger to the left and move it forward slowly until it meets the tip of the left index finger, which is pointing up.

YOU

(IS) BORN

Move the right hand, palm toward the body, so that it rests with its back against the left palm.

THIS

Hold both hands palm up, then lower them slightly.

DAY

Hold the left arm palm down across the front of the body. Form the letter "D," palm facing left and index finger pointing up, with the right hand and rest the right elbow on the back of the left hand. Move the right arm in an arc until the index finger points to the crook of the left elbow.

IN

Move the fingers of the left hand down into the right hand.

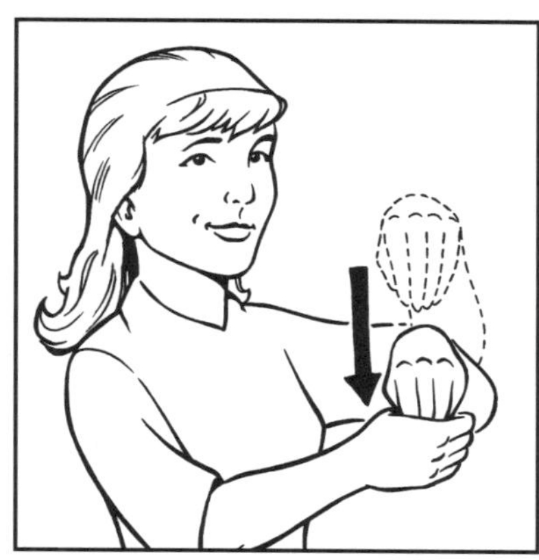

(THE) CITY

Form the point of a triangle with the fingertips of both hands. Separate and reconnect the fingertips a number of times to represent rooftops, moving the arms to the right each time the fingertips reconnect.

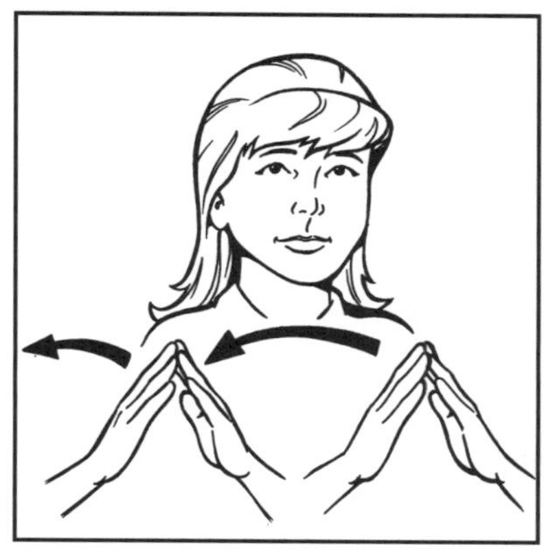

OF

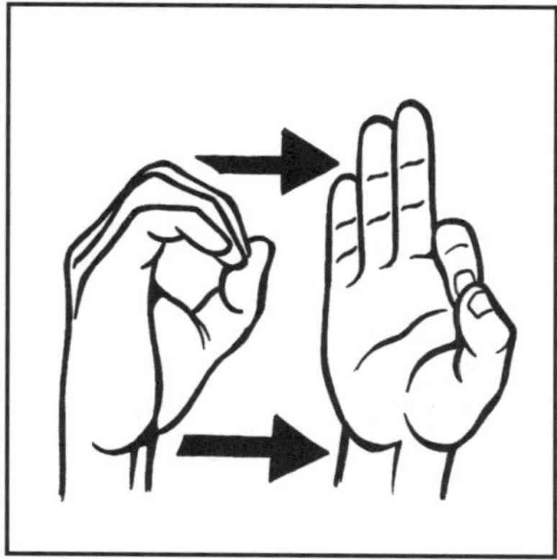

DAVID (KING DAVID)

Move the right "D" hand, palm facing left, from the left shoulder to the right hip.

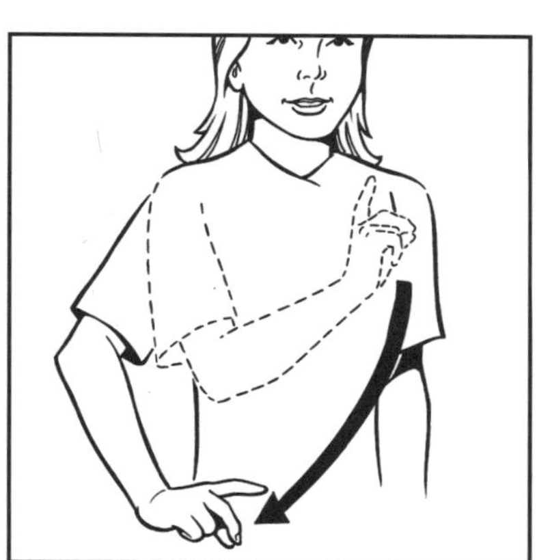

(A) SAVIOR

Hold both "S" hands in front of the chest, wrists crossed and palms facing in. Then pull both hands apart and away to shoulder level, palms facing out, as if pulled free from chains.

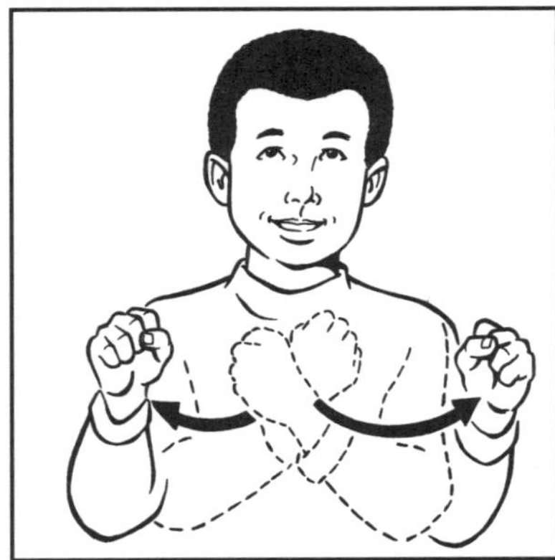

WHO

Make a small counterclockwise circle with the right index finger in front of pursed lips.

IS

Hold the tip of the right little finger to the lips, palm facing left. Move the hand straight out and away from the lips.

(THE) MESSIAH

The right "M" hand should touch the left shoulder then move down across the body to touch the right hip.

(THE) LORD

Hold the right "L" hand first at the left shoulder (palm facing left, index finger pointing up) and then down at the right hip (palm facing down).

In the beginning was the Word, and the Word was with God, and the Word was God.

IN

Move the fingers of the left hand down into the right hand.

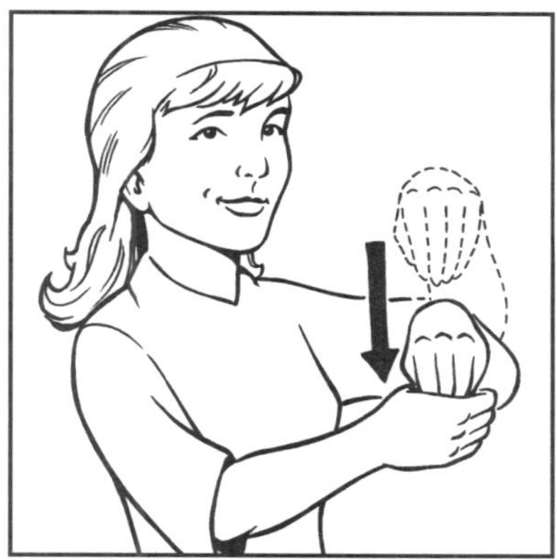

(THE) BEGINNING

Hold the left "5" hand with the palm facing the body, and place the right index finger, palm down, between the index and middle fingers of the left hand. Twist the right index finger to the right until the right palm is facing upward.

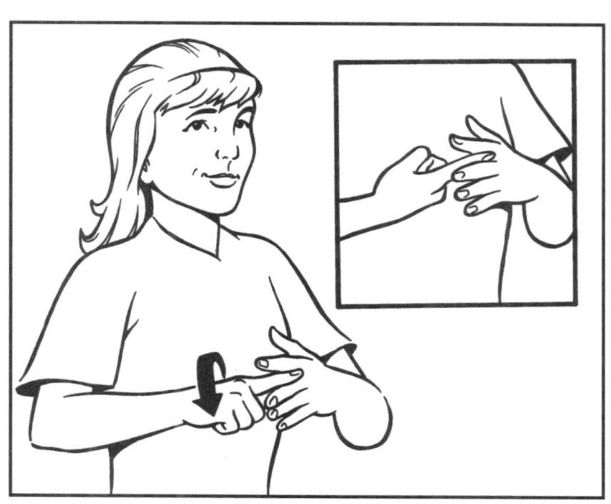

WAS

Raise the right hand to the right side of the face, palm facing the body. Curve the right hand back over the right shoulder.

(THE) WORD

Hold the left index finger up with the palm facing right. Place the thumb and index finger of the right hand "Q" against the left index finger.

AND

Hold the right hand out at chest level with the fingers slightly spread and the palm facing the left shoulder. Then pull the hand to the right while closing the fingers together.

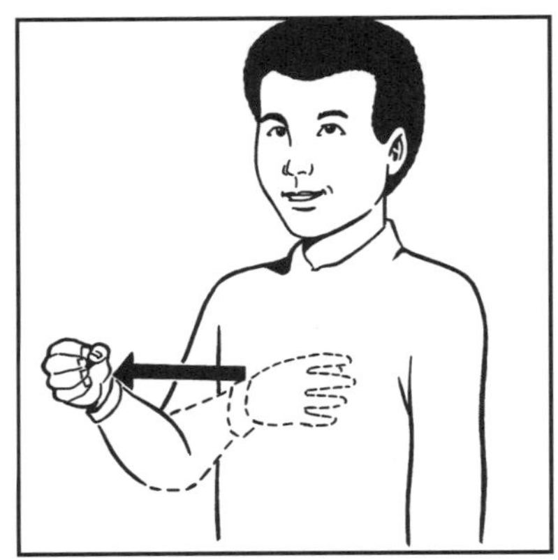

(THE) WORD

WAS

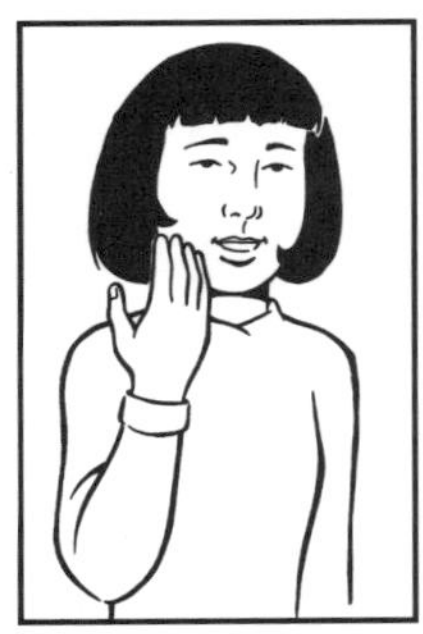 

WITH

Bring the two "A" hands together with the palms facing.

GOD

Make a "G" with the right hand, palm facing left, and point forward and up at head level. Then move the right hand down and back toward the body, ending with an open palm facing left at chest level.

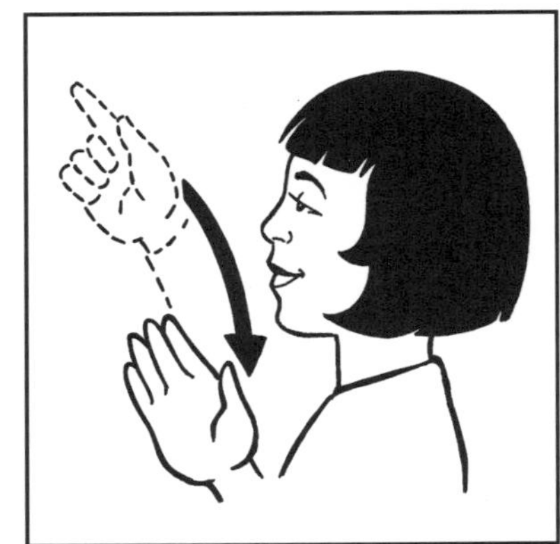

AND

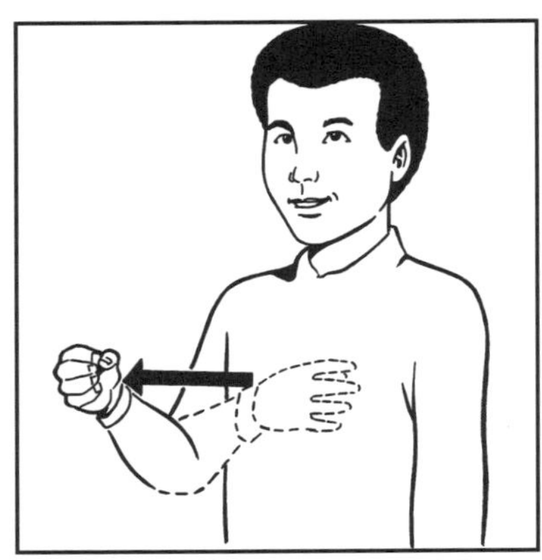

(THE) WORD

WAS

GOD

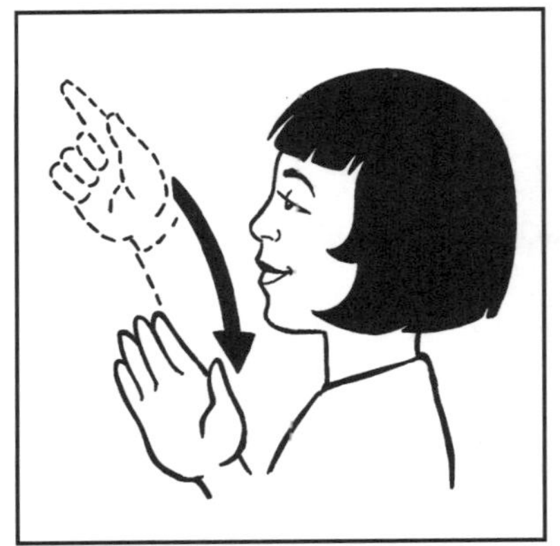

*For God so loved
the world
that he gave his only Son,
so that everyone
who believes in him
may not perish but
may have eternal life.*

(FOR) GOD

Make a "G" with the right hand, palm facing left, and point forward and up at head level. Then move the right hand down and back toward the body, ending with an open palm facing left at chest level.

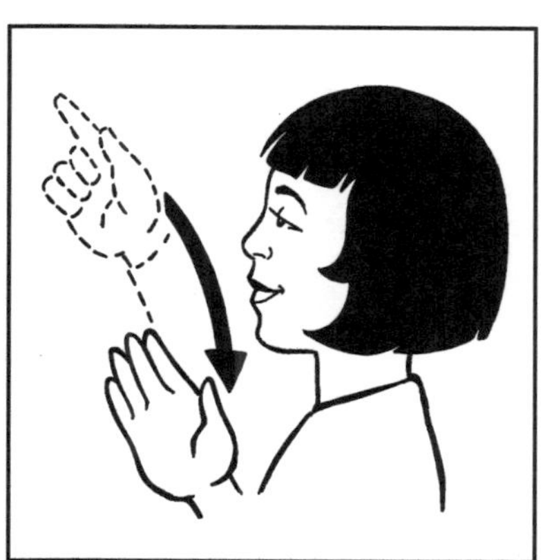

(SO) LOVED

Cross both hands at the wrists and press them over the heart.

(THE) WORLD

Bring the right "W" hand, palm facing left and fingers pointed up, in a circle over and around the left "W" hand, palm facing right and fingers pointed out.

(THAT) HE (GOD)

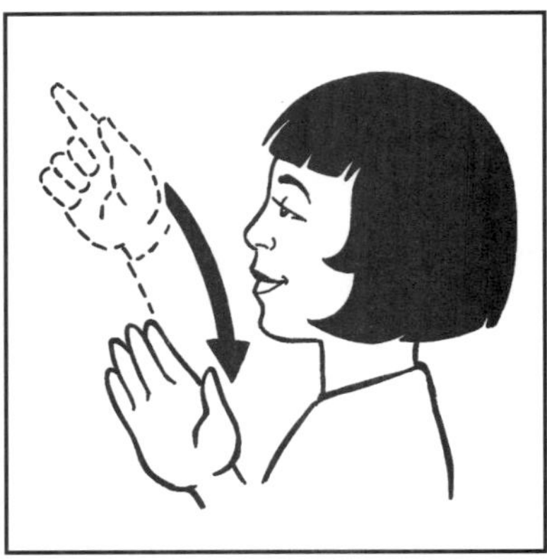

GAVE

Hold both hands in front of the body, palms up and fingers and thumb touching on each hand. Then pull the hands in to the chest.

HIS (GOD)

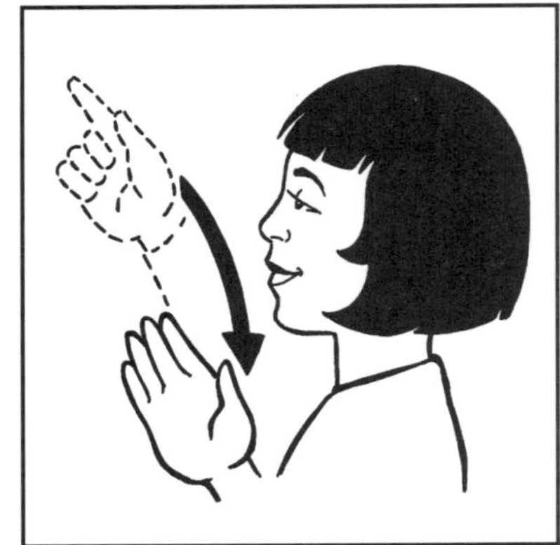

ONLY

Extend the index finger of the right hand, palm facing out, and then twist the hand to the left so that the palm faces the body.

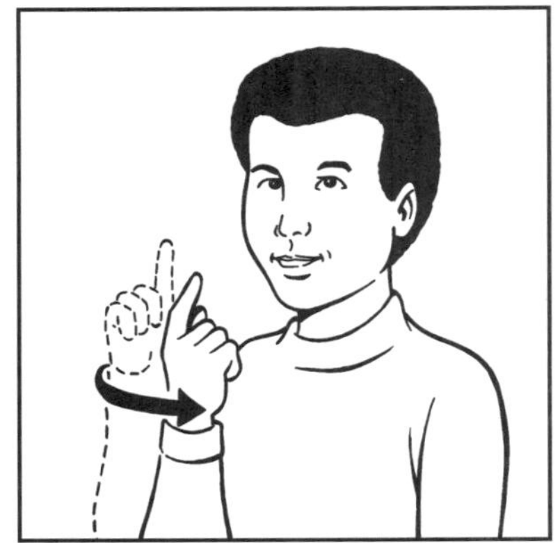

SON

Bring the thumb and extended fingers of the right hand to the right side of the forehead to grasp an imaginary cap brim. Then rock the arms together in the sign for "child."

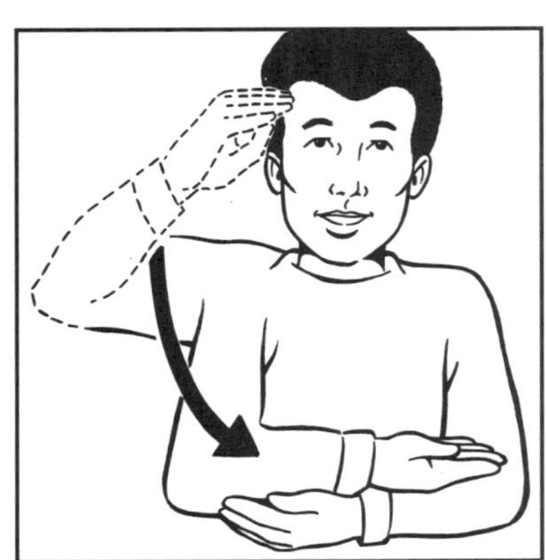

(SO THAT) EVERYONE

Make fists with both hands, thumbs out. Hold up the left fist and with the thumb of the right fist, stroke down the left thumb. Then move the right hand out and up with the index finger extended.

WHO

Make a small counterclockwise circle with the right index finger in front of pursed lips.

BELIEVES (IN HIM)

Touch the forehead with the right index finger. Bring the right hand down, palm flat, to meet the left hand, palm up, and clasp hands together.

(MAY) NOT

Place the right "A" hand under the chin. Move the thumb forward while moving the head from side to side, indicating "no."

PERISH

Hold the right palm up and the left palm down. Turn both hands over so that the right palm is down and the left palm is up.

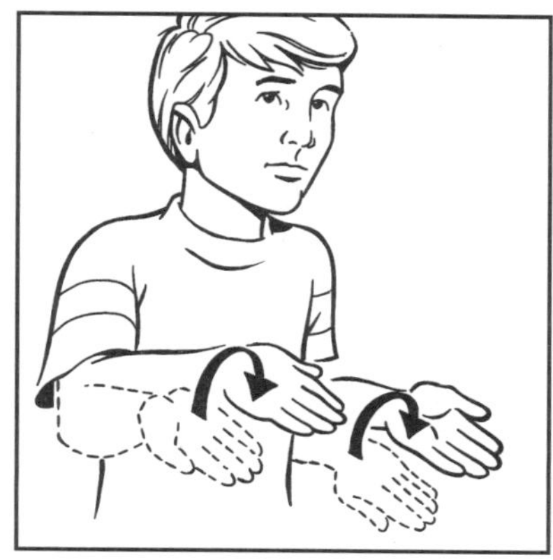

BUT

Cross the index fingers of both hands in front of the body, then pull the hands apart.

(MAY) HAVE

Touch the chest with the fingertips of both hands.

ETERNAL

With the right hand held palm up, use the right index finger to trace a clockwise circle in the air. Then, with the right hand palm down in the "Y" position, move the hand straight forward.

LIFE

Form an "L" with both hands, palms facing the body and index fingers pointed toward each other. Move both "L" hands higher up in front of the body.

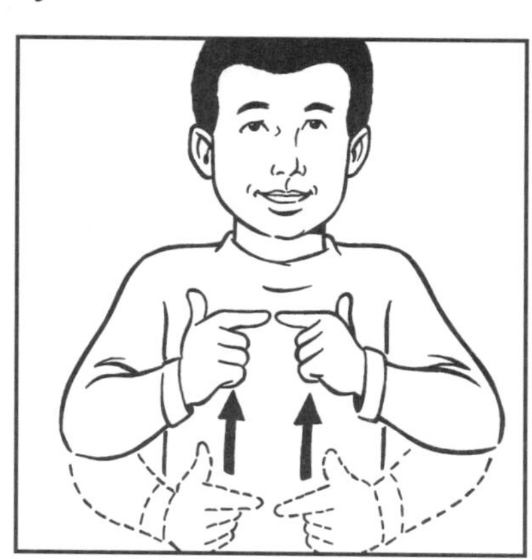

*Go therefore
and make disciples
of all nations,
baptizing them
in the name of the Father
and of the Son
and of the Holy Spirit.*

THIS IS KNOWN AS **THE GREAT COMMISSION.**

GO

Point the index fingers of both hands up, with one hand slightly behind the other. Then move both hands forward and down.

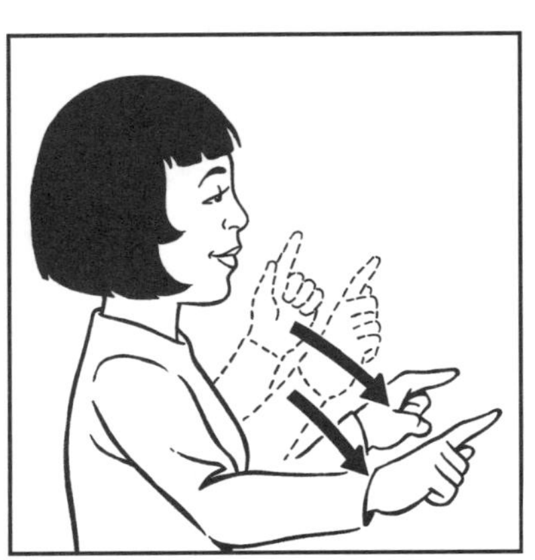

THEREFORE

Form a "D" with both hands, palms facing down and index fingers pointed forward. Together both hands make short arcs from right to left.

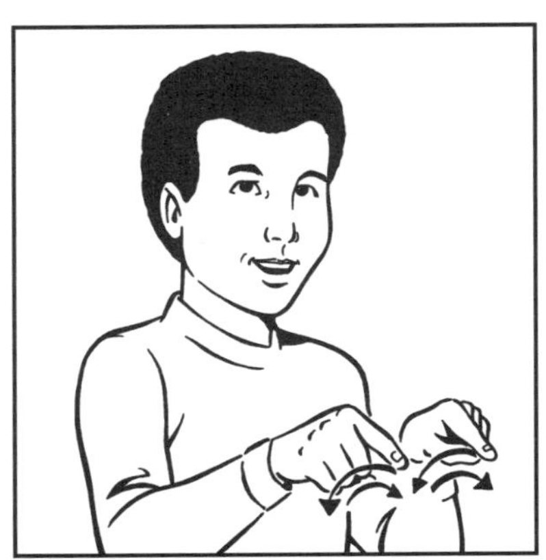

AND

Hold the right hand out at chest level with the fingers slightly spread and the palm facing the left shoulder. Then pull the hand to the right while closing the fingers together.

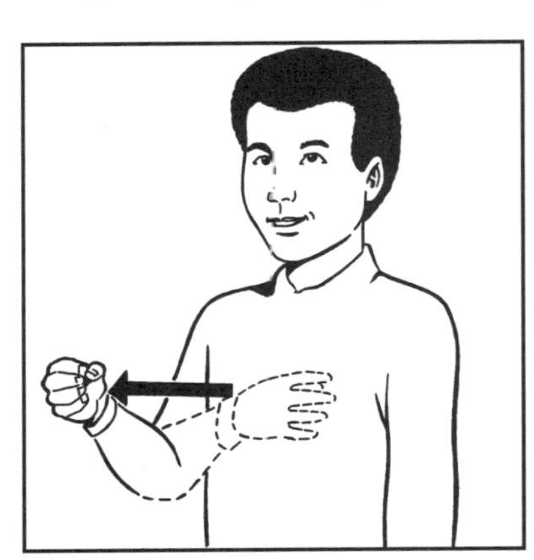

MAKE

Stack the right "S" hand on top of the left "S" hand, palms facing each other. Then twist the wrists in opposite directions.

DISCIPLES

With the left "D" hand in front of the right "D" hand, palms facing forward, move both hands forward simultaneously in double arcs.

OF

Use the right hand to spell the letters "O" and "F."

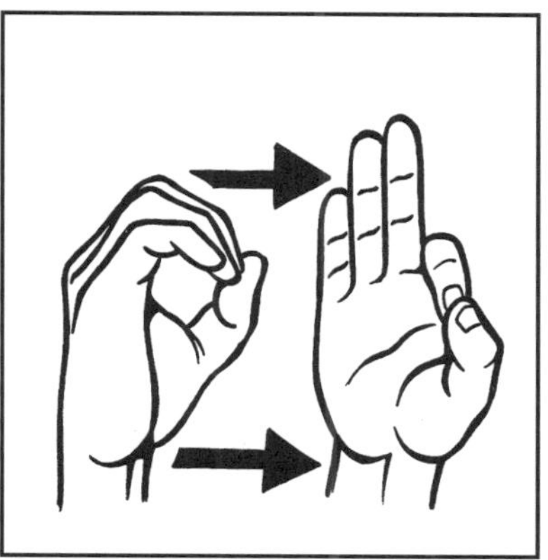

ALL

Hold the left palm facing the body. Circle the right hand, palm facing out, out and around the left hand. End with the back of the right hand in the open left hand.

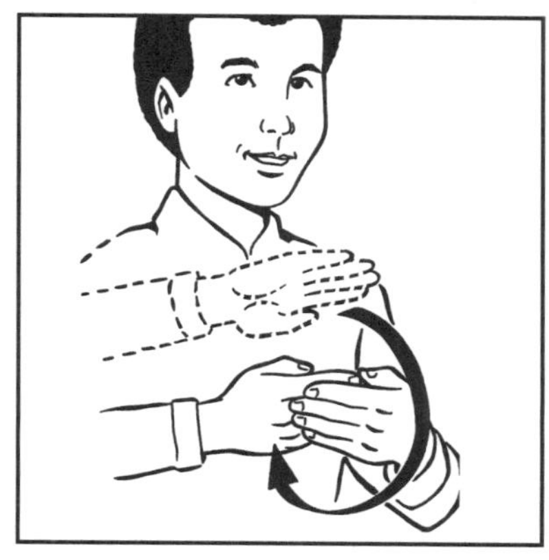

NATIONS

Hold the right "N" hand palm down and make a clockwise circle above the left hand. Then touch the back of the left hand with the tips of the right-hand "N" fingers.

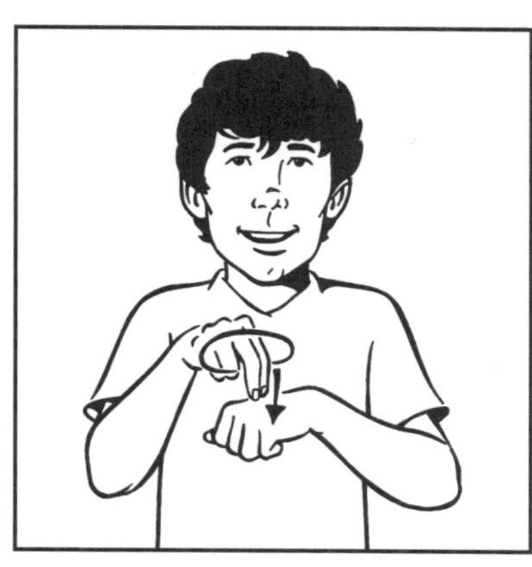

BAPTIZING

Tap the index finger of the right "W" hand, palm facing left, on the chin. Then hold the right hand above the right side of the head with the thumb and fingertips touching and the palm facing the head, and flick the fingers open as though sprinkling water.

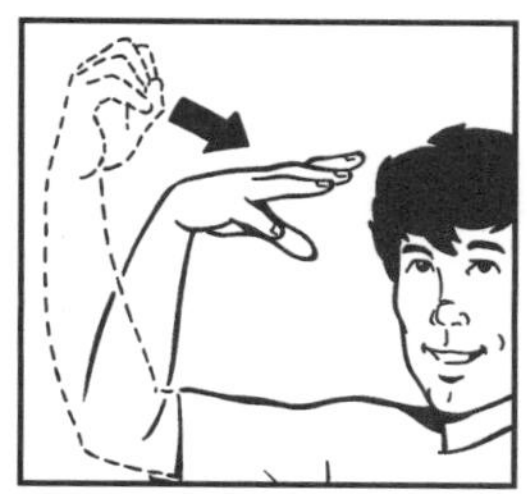

THEM

Point the right index finger to the left and then move it across the body to the right.

IN

Move the fingers of the left hand down into the right hand.

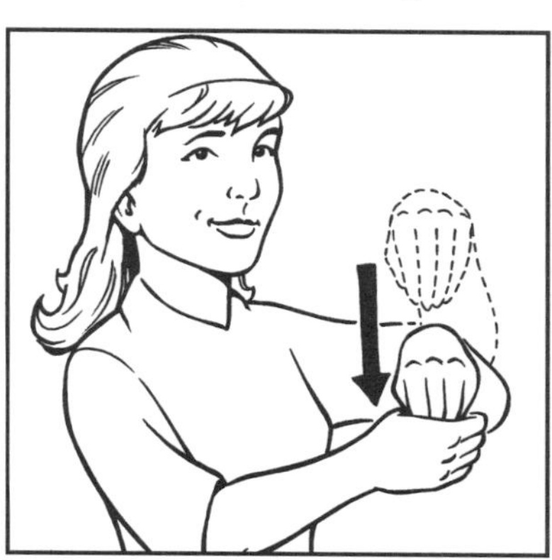

(THE) NAME

Both hands make an "H" and the index fingers cross, right hand on top, to form an x-shape.

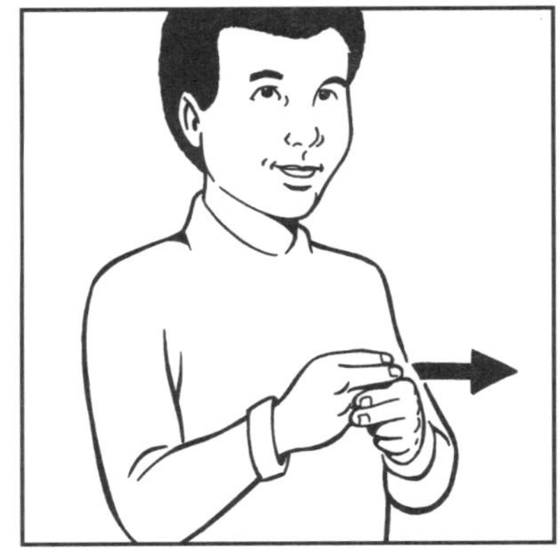

OF

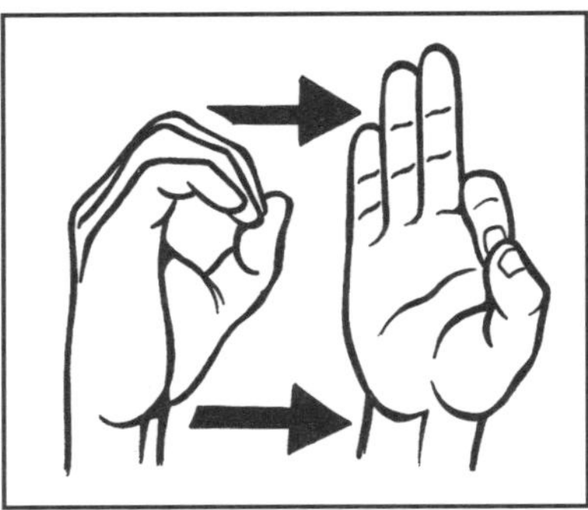

(THE) FATHER
(HEAVENLY FATHER)

Place the right "A" hand at the forehead with the palm facing left and place the left "A" hand out in front of the forehead with the palm facing right. Move both hands upward and outward toward the left while opening both hands into the "5" position.

AND

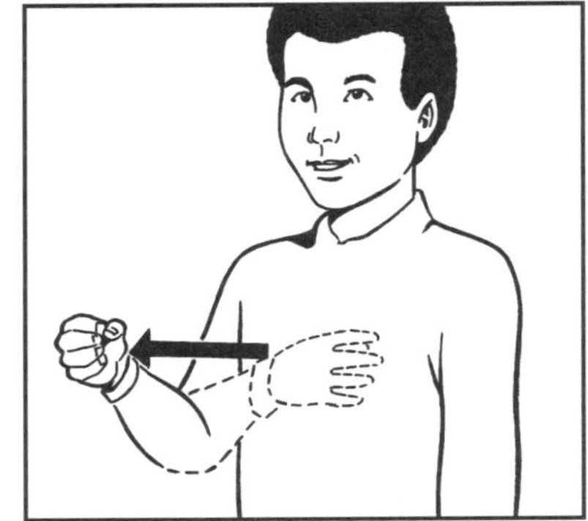

OF

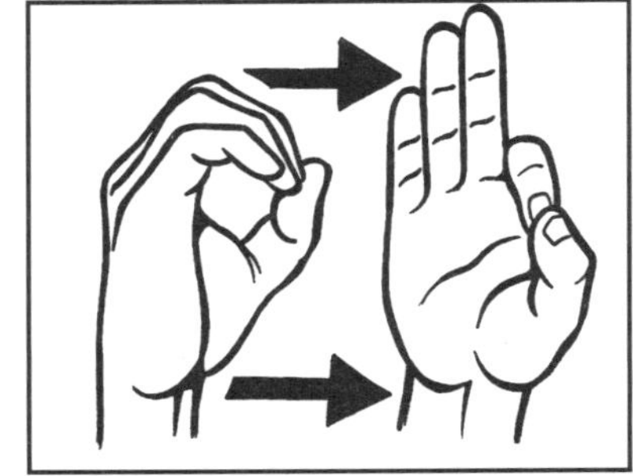

(THE) SON

Bring the thumb and extended fingers of the right hand to the right side of the forehead to grasp an imaginary cap brim. Then rock the arms together in the sign for "child."

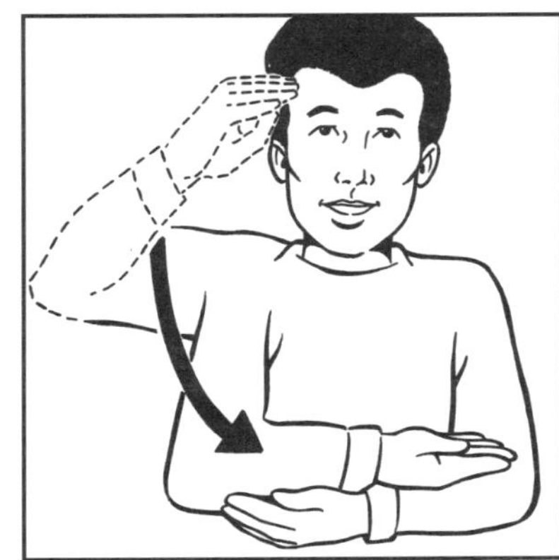

AND

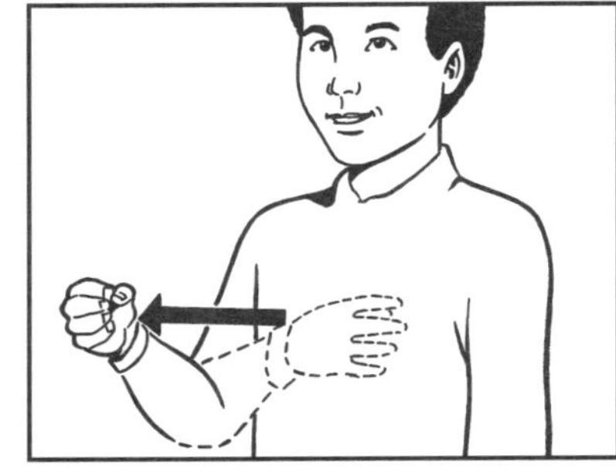

OF

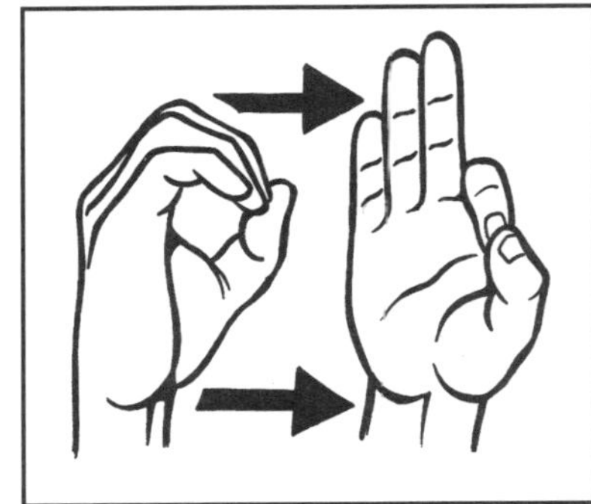

(THE) HOLY SPIRIT

Move the right "H" hand, palm facing left, in a small circle in front of the chest. Change to a flat right hand and wipe the palm of the right hand across the left palm from its base to off the fingertips, keeping fingers perpendicular to each other. Then touch the thumbs and index fingers of both "F" hands to each other, right hand over left and palms facing, and draw the hands apart.

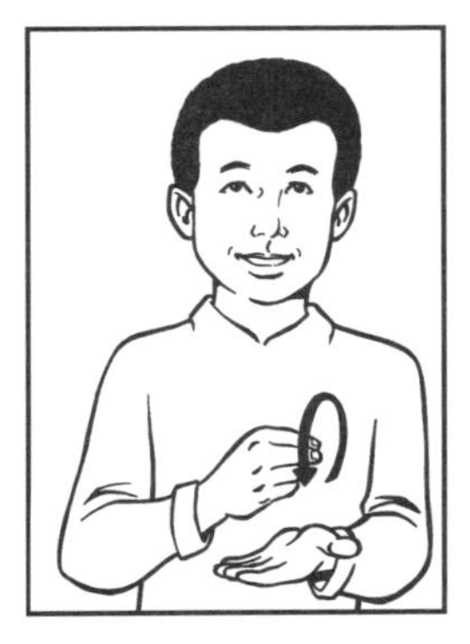
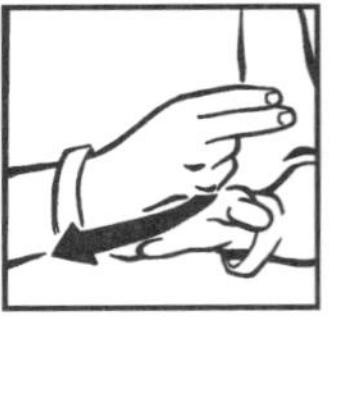

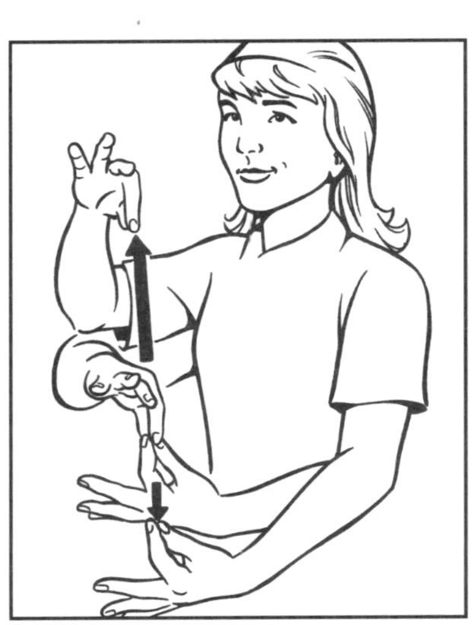

Now faith, hope, and love abide, these three; and the greatest of these is love.

FAITH (TRUST)

Touch the right side of the forehead with the right index finger, then move the right hand down, coming to rest in a fist on top of the left hand fist, palms facing.

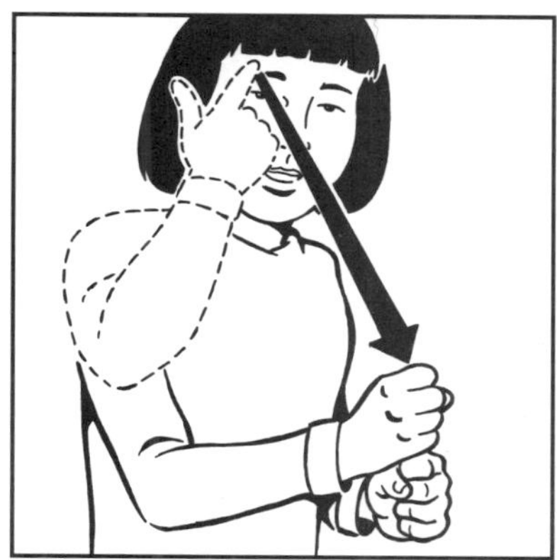

HOPE

Touch the right side of the forehead with the right index finger. Then move the open right hand out in front of the forehead. At the same time, raise the left hand near the left side of the forehead. Bend the fingers of both hands down.

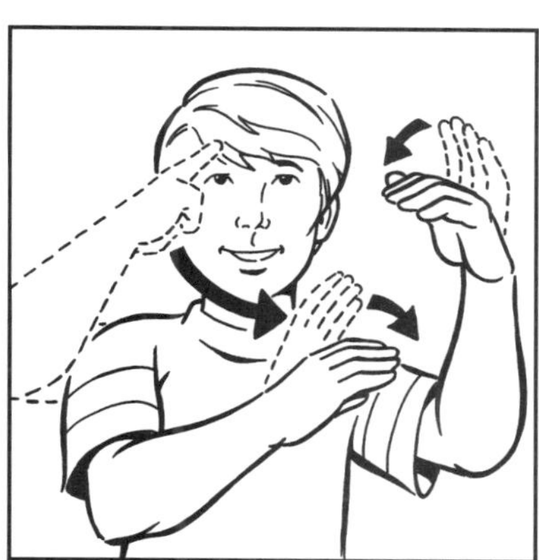

AND

Hold the right hand out at chest level with the fingers slightly spread and the palm facing the left shoulder. Then pull the hand to the right while closing the fingers together.

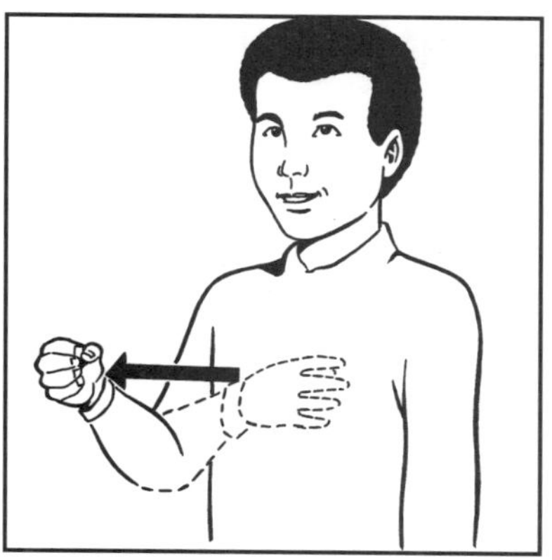

LOVE

Cross both hands at the wrists and press them over the heart.

ABIDE (STAY)

Hold the right hand in the "Y" position and move the hand down in a short movement.

THESE (THEM)

Point the right index finger to the left and then move it across the body to the right.

THREE

Hold up the thumb and the first two fingers.

AND

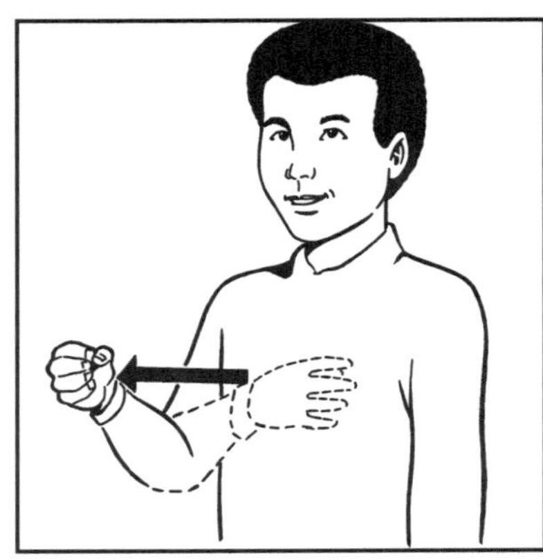

(THE) GREATEST (WONDERFUL)

With arms raised, hands open, and all fingers outstretched, pat the air repeatedly.

OF

Use the right hand to spell the letters "O" and "F."

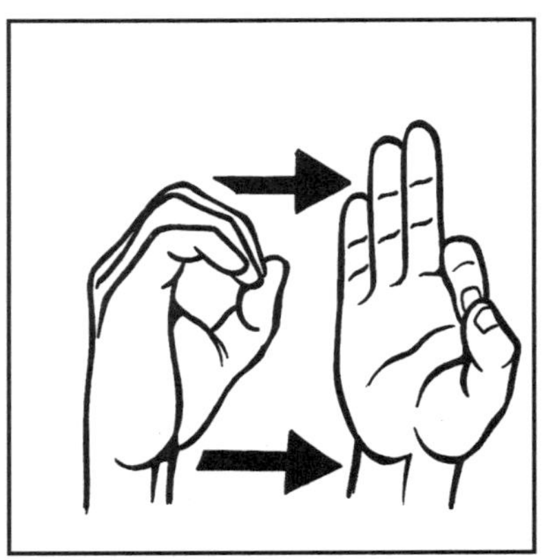

THESE (THEM)

IS

Hold the tip of the right little finger to the lips, palm facing left. Move the hand straight out and away from the lips.

LOVE

THE SEVEN LAST WORDS OF JESUS

Luke 23:34

Luke 23:43

John 19:26-27

Mark 15:34 (Matthew 27:46)

John 19:28

John 19:30

Luke 23:46

LUKE 23:34

FATHER (HEAVENLY FATHER)

Place the right "A" hand at the forehead with the palm facing left and place the left "A" hand out in front of the forehead with the palm facing right. Move both hands upward and outward toward the left while opening both hands into the "5" position.

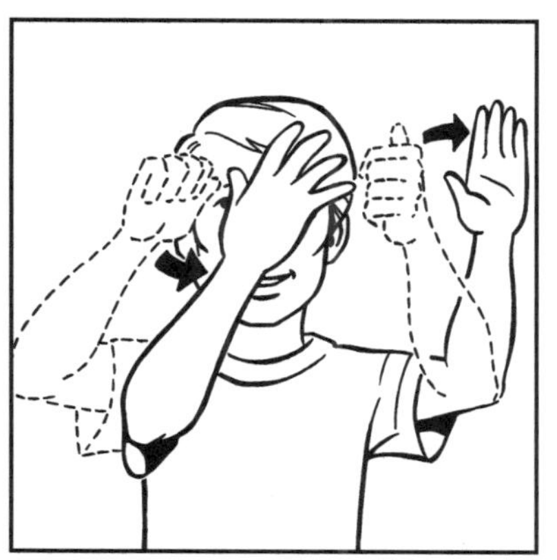

FORGIVE

Stroke the lower part of the left-hand palm with the right fingertips several times.

THEM

Point the right index finger to the left and then move it across the body to the right.

(FOR) THEY

Point the right index finger forward, then move it across the body to the right.

KNOW NOT

The right-hand fingertips tap the forehead several times. Then the right hand moves quickly over to the right, ending in the "5" position, palm facing out.

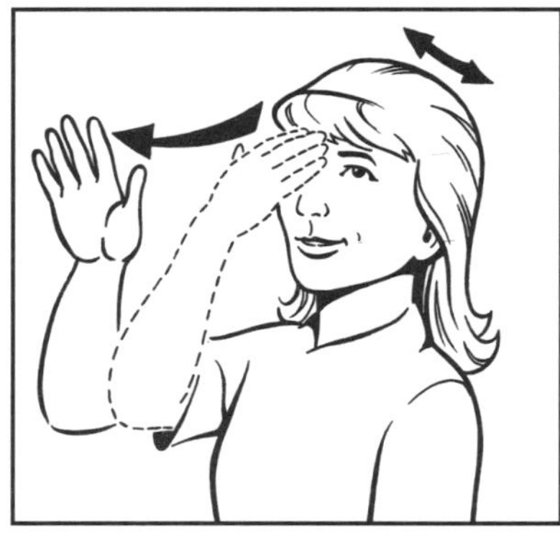

WHAT

Pass the right index finger over the fingers of the upturned left "5" hand, from the thumb to the little finger.

THEY

DO

Hold both "C" hands palms down. Move them simultaneously from one side to the other.

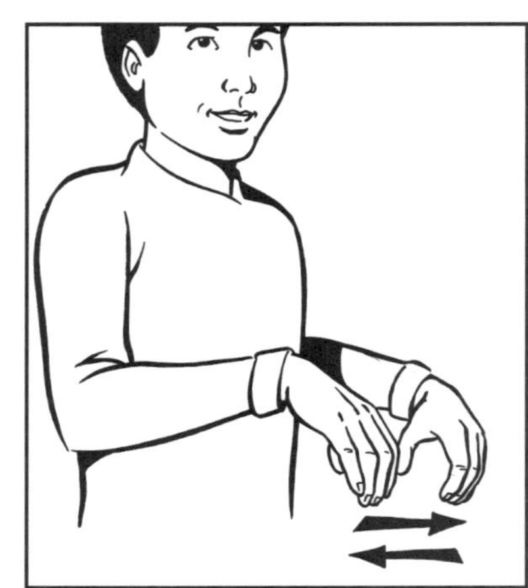

TODAY

Drop the upturned "Y" hands rather sharply in front of the chest. Then hold the left arm palm down across the front of the body. Form the letter "D," palm facing left and index finger pointing up, with the right hand and rest the right elbow on the back of the left hand. Move the right arm in an arc until the index finger points to the crook of the left elbow.

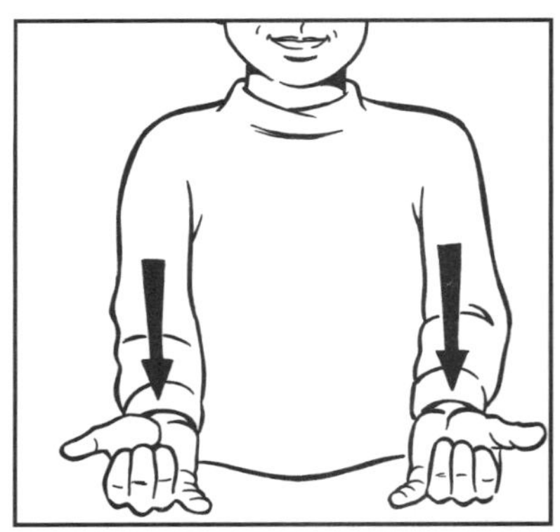

YOU

Point straight out in front with the right index finger.

WILL BE

Move the right hand, palm facing left, out and slightly up from a position beside the right temple. Then touch the "B" right hand to the lips and move it straight forward, away from the body.

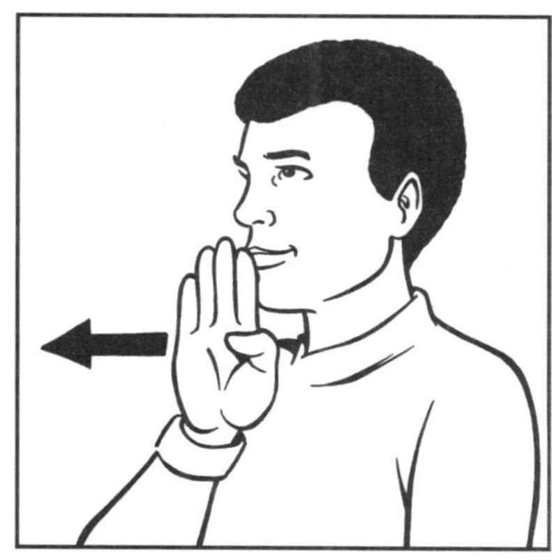

WITH

Bring the two "A" hands together with the palms facing.

ME

Point the index finger of the right hand toward the chest.

IN

Move the fingers of the left hand down into the right hand.

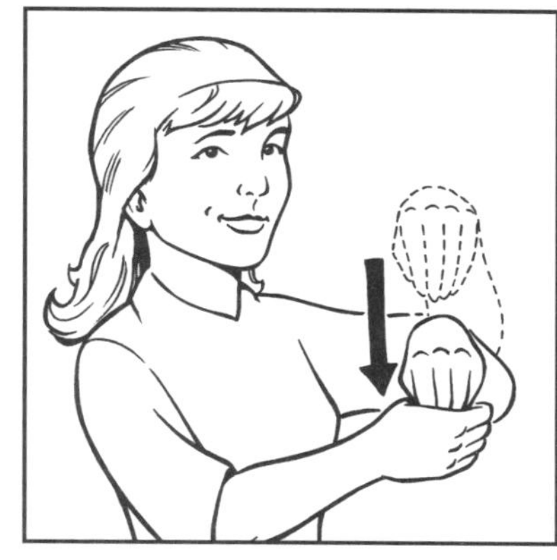

PARADISE (HEAVEN)

Bend both arms at the elbows and hold both hands with fingers together pointing straight up. Then move both arms together in an arc. Just before the hands touch, move the right hand palm down so that it sweeps under the left hand and then up, ending with the palm of the right hand facing out.

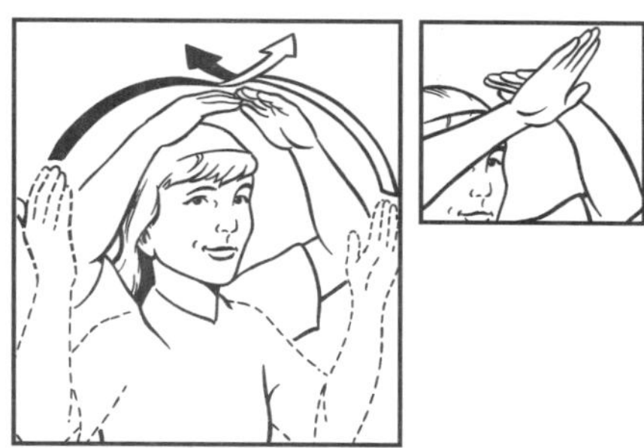

WOMAN

The right "5" hand is held first with the thumb on the chin, palm facing left. Then the right hand moves down to touch the chest with the thumb.

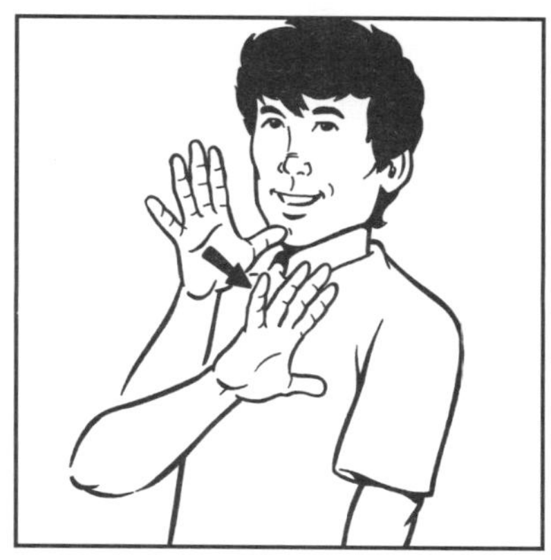

HERE

Make forward and outward circles with both hands, palms up.

IS

Hold the tip of the right little finger to the lips, palm facing left. Move the hand straight out and away from the lips.

YOUR

Hold the right hand up with the fingers pointed up and palm facing out, and push it forward.

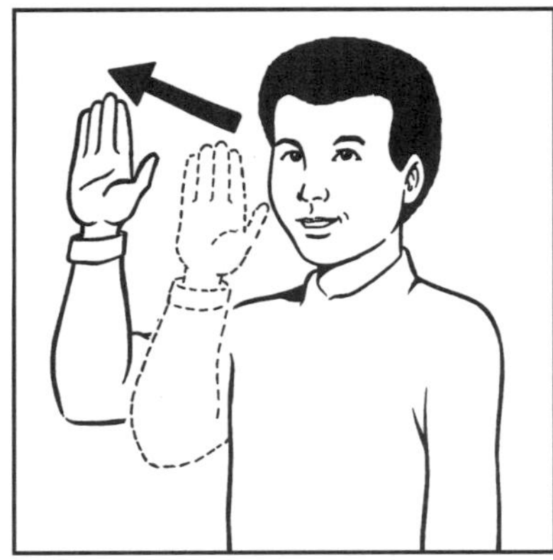

SON

Bring the thumb and extended fingers of the right hand to the right side of the forehead to grasp an imaginary cap brim. Then rock the arms together in the sign for "child."

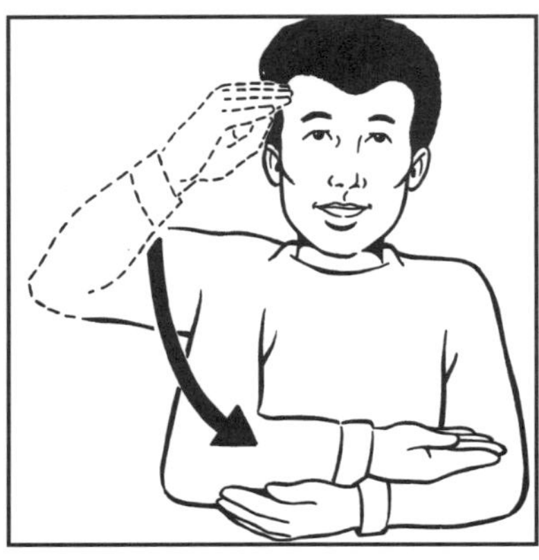

HERE

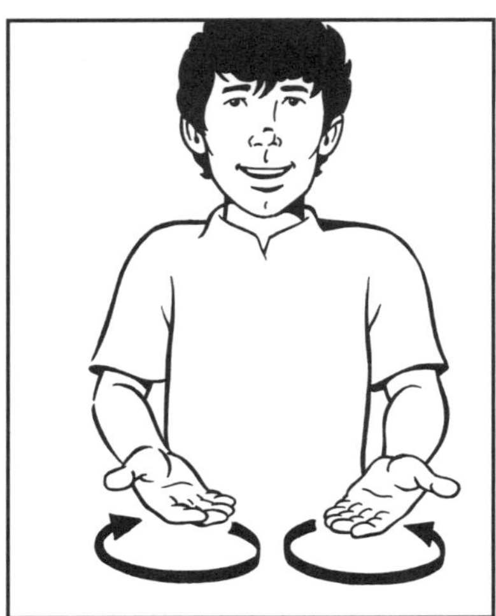

IS

YOUR

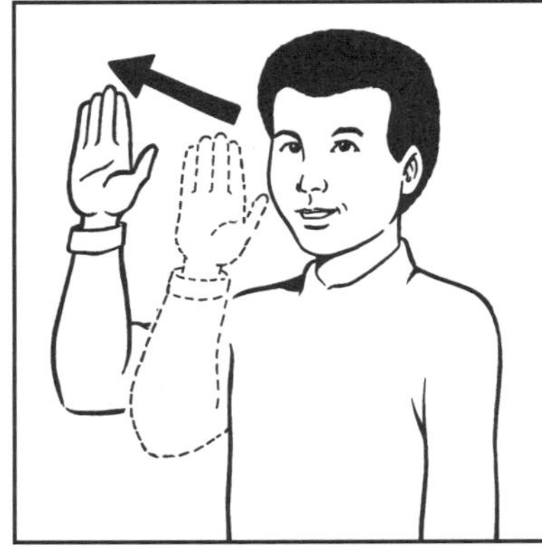

MOTHER

The thumb of the right "5" hand rests on the chin, palm facing left. Wiggle the other fingers slightly.

MY

Hold the "5" hand, palm facing in, against the chest.

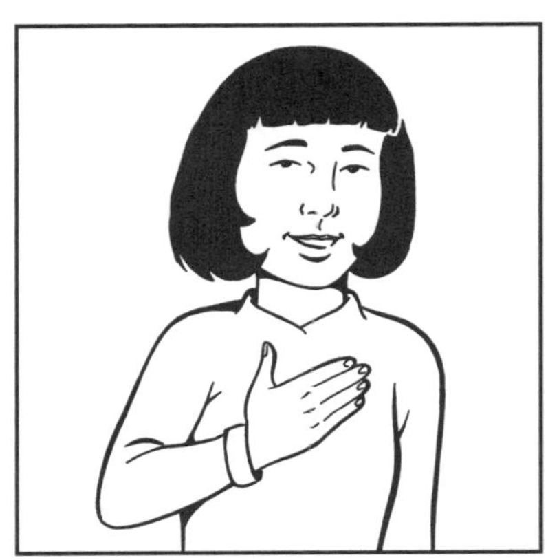

GOD

Make a "G" with the right hand, palm facing left, and point forward and up at head level. Then move the right hand down and back toward the body, ending with an open palm facing left at chest level.

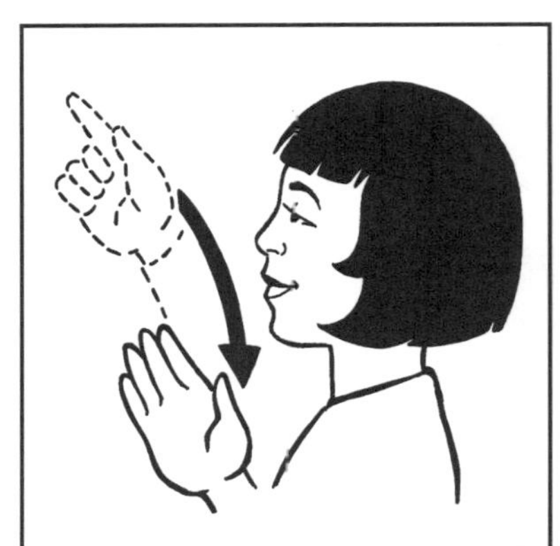

MY

GOD

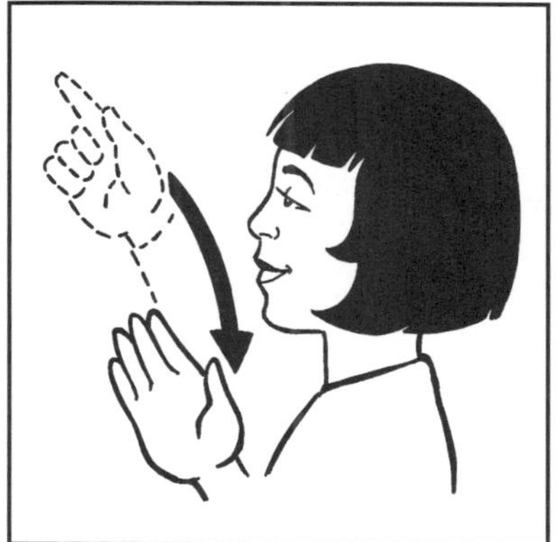

WHY

Hold the right-hand fingertips, palm facing the face, against the forehead. Then move the right hand to the chin and change the hand to the "Y" position, palm still facing the body. Facial expression is important to this sign, so be sure to look puzzled.

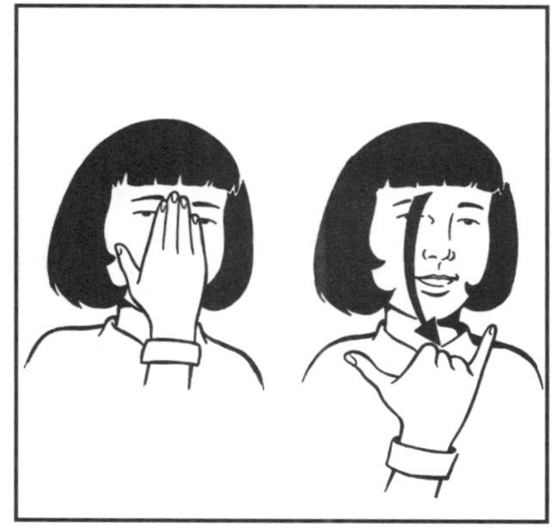

HAVE

Touch the chest with the fingertips of both hands.

YOU

Point straight out in front with the right index finger.

FORSAKEN

Place the right-hand palm on the forehead, fingers pointing left, and move it to the right across the forehead while closing into an "A" near the right side of the head. Then hold both "A" hands in front of the chest and thrust them forward, opening into "5" hands with the palms down.

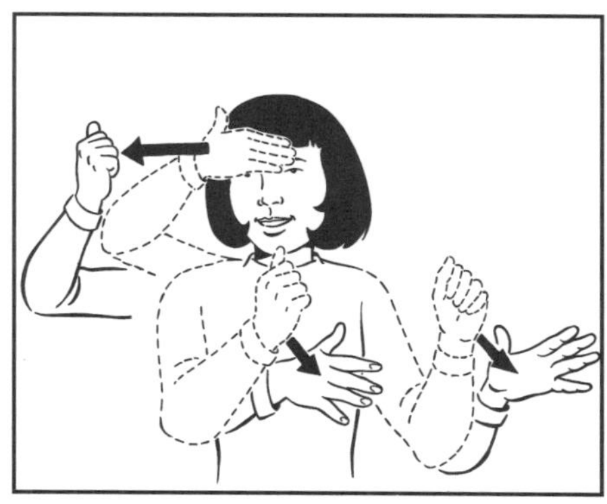

ME

Point the index finger of the right hand toward the chest.

I

Hold the right "I" hand with the thumb against the chest and the palm facing left.

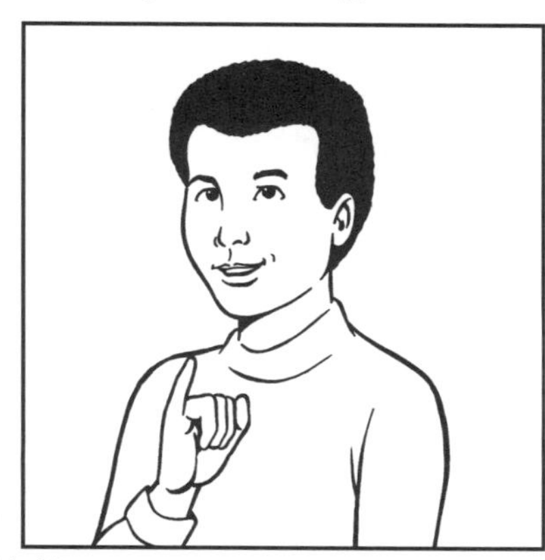

AM

With the right hand in the "A" position, palm facing left, hold the thumb at the lips and then move the hand straight out and away from the face.

THIRSTY

Trace a line with the right index finger that starts under the chin and ends near the base of the neck.

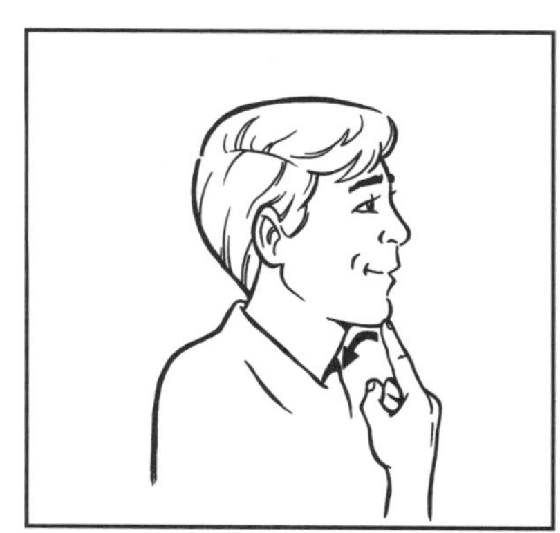

IT IS FINISHED

Hold both "5" hands with palms facing the chest and fingers pointing up, then twist the wrists sharply outward so that both palms are facing down.

INTO

Move the right hand down toward, behind, and under the left hand.

YOUR

Raise the right hand in the "5" position on the right side of the head, with the palm facing out. Move the hand up and away, toward heaven.

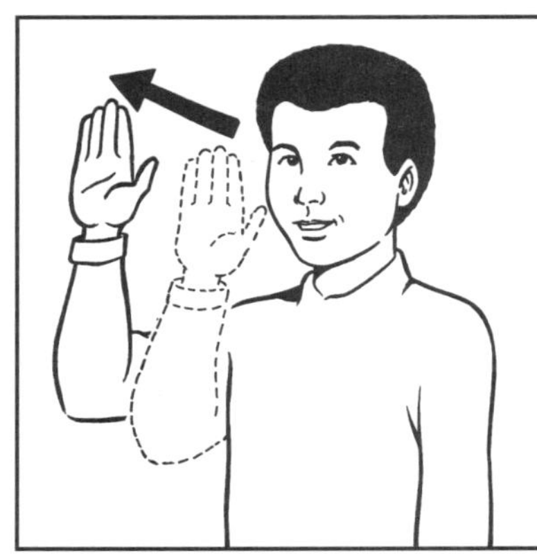

HANDS

With both palms facing down, place the right hand over the left hand. Move the right hand toward the body, and then repeat the action with the left hand over the right.

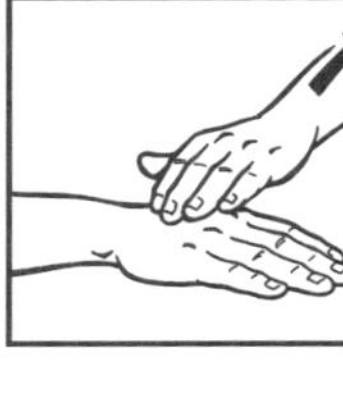

I

Hold the right "I" hand with the thumb against the chest and the palm facing left.

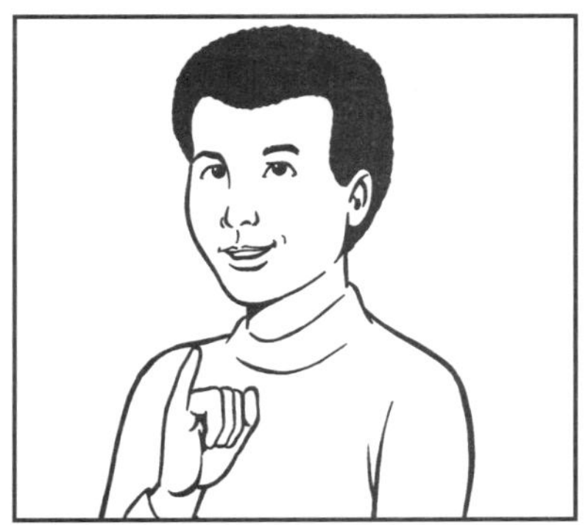

COMMEND (GIVE)

Hold both hands in fists, palms facing down, close to the chest. Then extend both arms away from the body with open hands, palm up. Make this gesture more grand than usual.

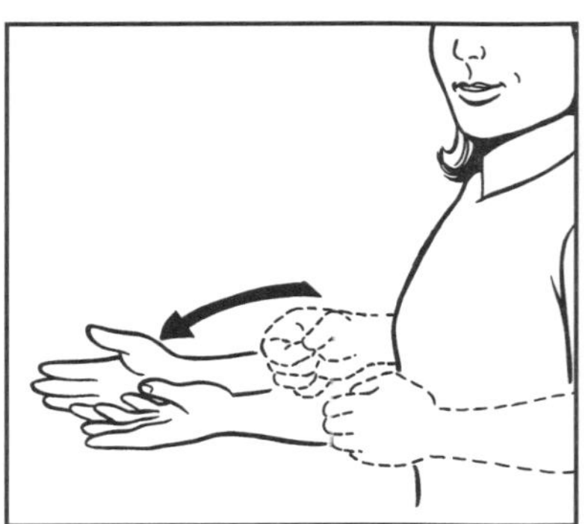

MY

Hold the "5" hand, palm facing in, against the chest.

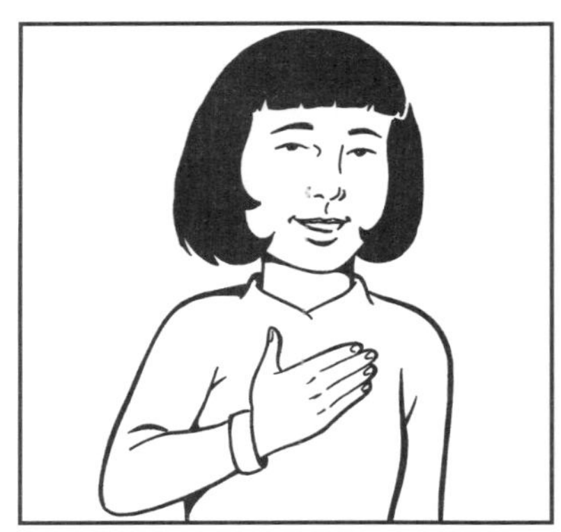

SPIRIT

Touch the thumbs and index fingers of both "F" hands to each other, right hand over left, palms facing. Pull the hands apart, lifting the right hand in front of the chest.

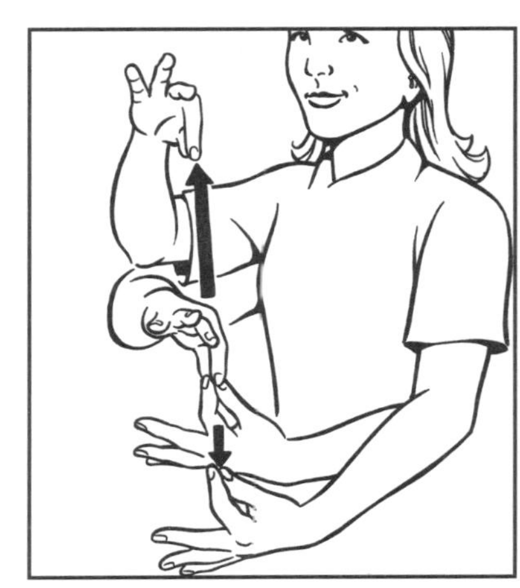

SCRIPTURE INDEX